SPIRITS IN THE FIELD

Bruce Hopkins
12/7/03

SPIRITS IN THE FIELD

AN APPALACHIAN
FAMILY HISTORY

Bruce Hopkins

Wind Publications
2003

First Edition

International Standard Book Number   1-893239-19-5
Library of Congress Control Number   2003106241

Cover photographs by Bruce Hopkins —
the Old Prater Cemetery shortly before its excavation.

Prologue

The voices in the house gently nudge him into wakefulness. Half-heard voices, half-dreamt perhaps, not immediately familiar, but not alien; somehow euphonious, like words from a long-forgotten nursery rhyme. The feather pillow cradling his head muffles them, if they are real at all. But they must be real, he thinks. He heard them speak.

And he has heard them before, somewhere in the gloaming region near sleep, where he has little defense. Sometimes just as he yields, or just as he breaks free, but always when the living senses are enervated and there is little to obscure those other senses, those not corporeal, those senses that yet have no place in his life.

The voices are nervous, anxious, as if they are debating something, something important. If he could open his eyes he could see them, he thinks, but he cannot move.

"You sure he's the one?" a voice asks. "How can he be the one?"

"Just watch," a second voice replies. "He'll do it."

"Don't look like much to me."

"You mark my words. He'll be there."

"Listen," says another anxiously. "You can hear them dig."

Dig? Dig for what? He struggles to listen, but when he does, he hears them no more.

He awakens, almost fully. There is the sound of a tiny shovel cutting into the glistening slack coal that rests in the dented bucket near the fireplace. It is usually his mother who does this as they settle in for the night, but he knows his mother is not

i

there. He recalls his father coming home from work today and rushing to the kitchen where his mother had filled up the wash tub for his bath. He remembers her doing her hair and laying out his father's best clothes on their bed and laughing happily as they dressed before climbing into his father's big green Packard and driving off into the evening.

It must be Mamaw, he thinks. Who's she talking to?

His grandmother attempts to be quiet as she banks the fire, but she knows if any of her grandchildren will hear her, it will be him. She hopes to feed the fire enough and cover it warmly with ashes so it will sleep until morning, as she hoped her grandson would after he had his supper and slipped into bed. But the boy is full of wonder, and has not long since stood at the window in the full March moon and watched the frost form on the new-plowed ground of the garden.

She had looked out the window herself before tending the fire, in worry for the new plants she put out today, and raised her hand to her lips with concern. He sees her gray hair, made nearly white by the bright spring moon, let down and free from her Old Regular Baptist mode. She's old, he thinks, and he wonders how old were the old folks she tells him about.

"Is somebody here, Mamaw?" he asks.

"What are you still doing up, baby?" she whispers gently, as she pats down the ashes in the fireplace. "Your brother and sissy are already asleep."

"Is Mommy and Daddy home yet?"

"Not yet," she says, completing her work. "They'll be back soon."

"I thought I heard somebody," he mutters. His eyelids are still heavy, and when he closes them, sleep beckons enticingly, calling him back to his dreams. He forces himself awake.

"Will you tell me a story?" he asks, to stave off sleep, and to absorb the warmth of his grandmother's voice.

"What kind of story you want to hear?" She dusts off her hands and wipes them on her apron before sitting down on the bed next to him.

"You want a 'Once Upon A Time' story?"

"No," he says petulantly. "That's for little kids. Tell me about the Old Ones."

He turns on his side, away from her and toward his younger brother who is softly, rhythmically breathing, already asleep, and he smiles in anticipation of the tale she will weave from the moonbeams swirling through the window. She knows he wants a 'Once Upon A Time" story anyway, and she lies on top of the cover next to him with one arm propping her gray head and the other across his body as he grasps the soft hand that reaches for his.

"Well, what do you want to hear?"

"Was Harlen one of the Old Ones?" he asks, sleep deliciously trespassing on his will to stay awake.

"No," she says sadly. "He was a young man. The Old Ones were gone a long time before he was born."

"Did they have cats, like Momsy and Peaches?" he asks, his ability to make sense, to form meaningful sentences dissolving, his eyes sealing themselves off in spite of his efforts, like the moon itself was his antagonist. In the protection of her arms here in the safety of his father's house, he has no more need for wakefulness, no need to guard against voices he is not yet ready to hear, and he is vanquished.

"Sure did, just like Momsy and Peaches. And dogs. Even ducks and gooses," she replies.

"Gooses?" he rasps. He had never seen a goose.

"Yep, they were farmers. Had all kinds of animals, but they didn't have mines then. Didn't have any work."

"Not like Daddy . . ." he barely breathes, and is unable to finish the thought. The moonlight and the sanctuary of his grandmother's arms have stolen it and he is unconcerned with the theft. He knows he will not hear the end of the story, but he is content. It is a ritual they have established, his grandmother and him, and he thinks it will always be so. He is at peace with the banked fire and the magic of his grandmother's words and the feather pillow and the warm quilt he sleeps under.

She begins: Once upon a time . . . Within a few words, he recognizes the tale.

I know this one, he wants to say, but cannot, will not, open his mouth. It is a good story, even if he has heard it, when his grandmother baby-sits or when he stays all night at her house. She speaks of people he never knew, but who were important, somehow, and he tries again to commit their names to memory. Strong men, beautiful women, and happy children; all gone. Triumph and tragedy, life and death, deeds unrecorded anywhere but in her words, or in her torn smile, which is the only expression he has ever known of her face.

And as she speaks, someone comes back into the room. Others follow, and they gather at the foot of his bed; he senses them there, but cannot open his eyes.

He wants to ask, who are these people, Mamaw? But they are quiet this time, not quarreling; listening instead as his grandmother speaks. They do not argue among themselves, do not argue about him.

Why'd they argue about me anyway, he wonders? Does Mamaw know they're here?

But he knows they are, even if tomorrow he will forget. They stand attentively, if imperceptibly, and he cannot will himself to acknowledge them to her. And then sleep, soothing and sweetly breaking, overtakes him.

He will be ten years old this year.

As she tells the story, she remembers herself at his age, when her grandmother first told it to her and she tells it completely, even though she knows he will not hear it all. But she continues, as if it is too precious not to be told in its entirety, as if she had an audience beyond her grandson to tell it to, as if she were again a child in her grandmother's house when she first recited the tale.

Her grandson is snoring easily when she is done and she presses her lips to his hair before getting up.

"I love you, baby boy," she says quietly. "I love all my babies," she says to no one in particular. "Everyone."

Soon it will be her birthday; she is only days away from fifty-two and cannot fathom how she has grown so old so rapidly. Alone, she returns to the living room, passing through the formless dust that quietly shimmers in the spring moonlight at the foot of the bed, and which parts obediently to let her pass.

In time, the child sleeping under the quilt she made for his father will himself be fifty-two.

When he reaches that age, she will have been twenty years in her grave.

When he reaches that age, his father will be gone as well.

When he reaches that age, as disconsolately as an orphan, he will find himself searching his memory for any fragment of her stories, any trace of the silver dreams she once spun so effortlessly around him, any clue to the mysteries she once so openly revealed to his childish heart.

And he will conclude, to his crushing sorrow, that he has forgotten nearly every legend she told him in childhood.

SPIRITS IN THE FIELD

PART I

The Strengthless Dead

Winter

Snow flurries skimmed along the car hood as we hurried through the starless night back to the hospital. We had barely gotten home when the call came, and we could still feel warmth in the car seats as we climbed back into them. It was expected. My brother told me earlier that he had whispered to my father that it was all right to let go; that he did not have to struggle anymore, that his children were all doing well, with good jobs and good futures, and they would always love him. But my father fought on as long as he could, as was his nature, against the cold pressing in at the window, against the blue chill seeping through his body, until he could fight no longer. When the disembodied voice said we were needed at the hospital, I knew it was over.

There was an old Marine who had taken up with my father in his last days, but he was gone when we got to my father's room. He learned my father had been a soldier, and hovered nearby these last few days, in hopes of sharing stories with him, comparing terrors of the same war they once fought on opposite sides of the world: the bitter cold of the Ardennes versus the rotting swamps of the Solomons. But my father did not recover, and the old Marine, in spite of his infirmity, assumed an ancient duty at my father's door, reporting as sentry one last time.

The doctors did what they could: the offending part was cut out, although it still throbbed when my father felt for the leg no longer there, but by then it was purely mathematical. The whole was now less than the sum of its parts, and it was not enough. When my father's spirit dismissed him from his post, the old Marine retreated to his room, giving up my father's body to his family in their grief. With his duty done, in the loneliness of the survivor, he watched the winter night close in on him as he added another face to the long parade of comrades he would never see again.

But the weather, so ugly and grim during the deathwatch, changed the day we buried my father. It seemed like early spring, like a beginning instead of an end. Unusually warm for the first week in January, too late for Indian summer and even warmer than the usual winter thaw that sets in after Christmas, on the day of his burial, Gardner Fork of Greasy Creek was flooded with sunlight.

I took off my jacket as I walked across the road from my brother's house to my parents' house. I was born in that house and I had hoped my father would spend his last days there instead of the antiseptic hospital room that was his death chamber. He would have preferred that too, but one rarely picks the place of his death.

I broke a sweat from the effort, and I wondered how it could have become that warm so suddenly, since the previous week had been so cold.

Our family had gathered at the house on this last day we would see my father's face, and we would all drive to the funeral together. The windows were opened to admit the breeze, and the drapes stirred quietly in the awesome stillness of the living room.

My parents' house was a tiny six-room structure with a fine brick chimney no longer used. It originally had only two rooms, and was built with whatever materials were available in the scarce days after the end of World War II. There were three or maybe four types of gypsum board on the walls, the result of purchases made of necessity when lumber or nails or Sheetrock was snapped up as soon as it went on sale. There were other soldiers who had returned after the war, and they were building houses too. The boys of Greasy Creek who survived the war

4

were hungry to start their lives of peace, and building materials, regardless of whether they matched, were at a premium.

Over the years, my parents had closed in the porches and added a bathroom, and it looked much like any other small house on Greasy Creek, but our house had a history. It was the second house built on the site and only Hopkins' were raised there. To this day, the house draws its water from the well my great-grandfather sank nearly a hundred years ago.

Harrison Hopkins dug the well and built the first house with sawn wood instead of the logs that were still the common building material of the day. He built a barn and cleared the land around the house for gardens. When he was done, his mother, Dorcus Hopkins, gave her final approval by planting a sapling from the great pale pink rose bushes she grew at her own home. This would bring joy to the house, she told him, and to ensure longevity and remembrance, she planted a cedar tree near the rose.

Harrison moved his family into the house and lived there until Lila, his wife, died during the Great Spanish Influenza Epidemic. He then gave it to his children, and it provided shelter for other Hopkins generations for decades. I might have been born in the house had not my great-aunt, Pearl Adkins Hopkins, set it on fire one sultry afternoon.

She did this after nailing all the doors and windows shut to prevent the escape of her husband, my great-uncle Jesse. He was the youngest of Harrison's boys, and although he lived in the house with Pearl, she was away that day and he mistakenly thought it would be safe to bring one of the less virtuous ladies of Greasy Creek home with him. But Pearl arrived home unexpectedly and, observing the partially-clad woman in question dashing out the back door, decided to teach Jesse a lesson. He escaped the fire and the couple reconciled, as they usually did. Unfortunately, the house was destroyed, and its mournful ruins lay untouched for years. Harrison would not rebuild it, and when he was asked, he merely said he would live in his children's homes.

My father bought out the family interests in the property after the Second World War and built his own home on the site. My brother and sister and I would invariably elicit tales of Jesse and Pearl from the family when we found a piece of melted glass from the old place while playing under our big front porch.

Although my parents' house was small, where Harrison's was much larger, there were often visitors, family from out of town who remembered the old place and could somehow see it standing there near the cedar, which survived the fire. And Dorcus' massive pink rose bush still gave off its aroma on late summer evenings. The visitors would sit on the porch and rock in one of the old cane-bottom rockers that were rescued, or gently move with the porch swing as they talked of the old days.

Those were soft times, the Irish would say, as the family settled in for the evening and listened to the murmurs, the half-recognizable bits of conversations from other front porches up and down the hollow. It was a summer ritual, and there were always dulcet voices wafting along the creek that flowed alongside the perfume from Dorcus' roses as other families retired to their own homes to watch the light dim and fail.

For decades they sat there, on the porches of the old house or the new, and monitored the voices that recited the litany of life on Greasy Creek. The visitors were fewer when we boxed in the porch for new bedrooms, but by then the era of quiet evenings had passed. By the 1960's, the hollows were full of children and bedroom space was cleaved from any source. Everyone, it seemed, all up and down the creek, was too busy to sit and watch the daylight pull away from the mountain ridges or catch fireflies in June or listen to the creek tumble down the hollow on its inexorable journey to the sea.

The family was gathered in the house when I went in, and light was streaming through the windows, spreading across the kitchen table, as it did in my youth, when, as the first child, I had the chair to my father's right. My mother always sat across from me, and my brother sat to my right. My sister's chair was never certain; she usually sat on a corner between Mom and Dad or sometimes between Mom and my brother, and she suffered from the lack of place often accorded the youngest child. But there was no scrambling for place on that day: the man was not there to assume the head of the table.

"Are we ready?" I asked no one in particular, but since I was the oldest child, I had the responsibility to make the announcement. There was little to be said: it was time to go to the funeral home.

In the old days on Greasy Creek, funerals were at home, and were a curious commingling of joy and sadness as distant relatives came in from wherever they had emigrated over the years. Because it was larger, my grandmother Rissie Prater's house, one of the old coal camp houses, was most commonly used for Hopkins funerals. Our house was too small for such services, and until my father died, there had been no need. There had been only Lila's funeral in the previous house, for Harrison died a decade after Jesse and Pearl's incendiary conflict brought it to the ground.

When he passed away, he was living with Rissie, who at that time was a Damron, and lived in a small house just up Snake Branch Hollow, within sight of Harrison's place, now in ruins. She had built her house close to her father, like all Harrison's children had, but that house was also too small for a funeral, and the Old Regulars, of whom Harrison was one, preached his funeral outside in Rissie's yard, under a great buckeye tree that still stands.

The Old Regular Baptist Church was also in charge of my father's funeral, although he was not a member, and as is usual at their services, there was little empathy in their rigid view of salvation. One preacher, who had grown up with me and knew my father's many kindnesses, expressed his fervent hope that my father had received the Lord before he died, but most of them merely threatened the assembled mourners with the Church's usual admonition to repent or spend eternity in Hell. It was a harsh doctrine, and had reduced the membership of the church to a fraction of what it had been when I was a child.

At my father's wake the night before we buried him, some members of the church revealed this unforgiving creed by leaving the chapel when my father's Masonic brothers came in for their ritual goodbye. It was something I knew the more zealous would do and I thought I was prepared for it, but the hard slap of their intolerance still shocked me. Consequently, I sat in blind hatred for the ignorance of my race, and I can remember practically none of the preachers who held forth from behind his casket.

We passed the churchhouse on the way out of Greasy Creek that day, and I had lost little of the bitterness I had accumulated the night before. In that modest building, the departed elders of the church looked down on the congregation from old pictures on the walls, and I doubted any of them would fail to accept my father when he came. Something told me that the tenets of the church of today were different from when it was organized in 1871, when the bitterness of the Civil War was still palpable. It could not have lasted so long with such intransigence; it had to have been formed in brotherhood.

At the mouth of Greasy Creek, we crossed the Big Sandy River, where my father taught us to fish before the river became choked with garbage and coal waste. Over the past decade, it had become much cleaner, but it was no longer the river of my youth and was nothing like the river of my father's youth. But I regretted that he had been taken directly to the funeral home after he died, and had not had one last crossing of the river where we once pressed dough balls onto hooks to lure catfish onto our trot lines.

After the funeral service, we went to the cemetery, where a Disabled American Veterans Honor Guard waited. They were mostly old World War II soldiers like my father, assembled to render a final salute to Private First Class Marvin E. Hopkins, who fought under Patton, and the sunlight was glorious. Birds ventured song from the trees and yellowjackets buzzed, as if to offer him a welcome, and a soft breeze played over the rolling hills of the vast cemetery, which was almost new by graveyard standards, having been created only thirty years before. There were seats awaiting us beside my father's open grave.

After a final word from the minister, kinder now in that garden of the dead than when he had the host of his church surrounding him, the honor guard of old soldiers took over. My mother and my sister twitched when the DAV fired their volleys, but my brother and I heard the commands and were motionless as the rifles discharged. After Taps, the ceremony was over and I collected the expended brass from the rifles and distributed them among the men in the family who came.

One of them went to Caudill Robinson, a cousin, and the son of my great-aunt Bessie Hopkins Robinson, Jesse's twin sister. She was the only living child of Harrison, and Caudill, of all the other men at the funeral, was closest to my father. Caudill considered him his older brother, as did the rest of his cousins; they always referred to him as 'Brother.' Caudill was shorter than my father, who was shorter than me, but he had the aura of a much larger man. Marvin had always been his idol, and when Caudill won the Silver Star in Korea the person he wanted most to share it with was Marvin. Caudill understood the symbolism of the shell casing I gave him and he trembled slightly as he stared at it before reverently placing it in his pocket.

With everything done that we could have done, we began to walk back to our cars, but I found it difficult to pull away. It was not because I was unable to give up my father; I had long ago accepted his impending death. He had survived the war, but his battlefield surgery and the peritonitis that followed gave him diabetes in his later years. The loss of his leg was the final blow to his now weakened constitution. I watched his decline daily, but that was not the reason I found it hard to leave.

There was something missing in the service or the arrangements perhaps, but I could not quantify my misgivings. *What had we neglected to do?* I could not put my finger on what was troubling me. It had been a typical graveside service; all the protocols had been observed, but I felt something had been forgotten or left out. I had been to many funerals in this cemetery; it was undoubtedly the best of any in Pike County, and my father's funeral was as beautiful as any held there, but there was something wrong.

I put the feeling aside as we entered our cars to return to my parents' house.

On the trip back up Greasy Creek, we again passed the Old Regular Baptist church house, and my anger had waned. I was never a member of the church and would never be, but I could not deny my affection for my family and they were all Old Regulars. And there were memories of other funerals inside that unornamented structure or on the Old Prater Cemetery where the church would meet in summer months. Somehow death was more palatable there, where the mourners were augmented by an assemblage of tombstones. On boards held up by flat rocks, the congregation would sit as the preachers shouted from a decaying wooden stand.

Meetings on the Old Prater were discontinued in 1971, a hundred years after they began, and a new cinder block stand, built for the elders, had never been used. Perhaps I began my disassociation with the church from that time. I preferred the Old Prater to the churchhouse for the services my grandmothers would compel me to attend, since I could easily break away from them and explore the gravesites of my ancestors. Until recently, when new churches sprang up as the members hardened their stance, the Greasy Creek Old Regular Baptist Church was almost the only church to attend. Aside from occasional Catholic services rendered to the foreign workers in the Greasy Creek mine when it was open, it was the only church on Greasy Creek for a hundred years, except for the Primitive Baptists, who split from the fold in 1895 and claimed the same genesis.

At the forks of Greasy Creek, above the schoolhouse field, the Old Prater Cemetery, where most of the faithful of Greasy Creek once worshipped, sat quietly, facing the east and waiting for the Resurrection that was sure to come. I thought for a moment that I should go up and tell my grandfather that his son was gone, but I knew he knew. Besides, the Old Prater had always been there and would always be there, and I could share my sorrow with my ancestors some other time.

Later that day, when I went back to inspect the gravediggers work, I realized what had bothered me since the funeral service. As I walked between the symmetric rows of headstones to the fresh mound of dirt above his vault, I discovered something unusual for my father, who had always lived best with his family nearby: there was no family here to welcome him; my father would lie among strangers.

The Annie E. Young Memorial Cemetery, where my father was just buried, was a modern, well-maintained, perpetual care cemetery, and the graves were neatly laid out between smooth lanes that discreetly brought the visitor to his relative's plot. We owned eight plots. My father and my mother, Pansy Prater Hopkins, their children and their spouses were assured that his grave, and ours, would be tended forever, unlike the Old Prater, which was gradually succumbing to weeds and brush.

Eventually, my brother Paul and his family, and my wife Charlene and I would lie on the Annie E. Young as well. Charlene's own father would die the following year and would be buried nearby. My sister's first husband was already buried in the same cemetery and a plot was reserved for her, but now there were only strangers buried near my father. I knew nobody buried nearby, and my mother said she knew only one family. There were no kinfolk here, and my father would lie alone, away from the Old Prater, the cemetery he tended for his entire life, away from the graves and attendant spirits of his father and his grandfather, and away from the ghosts of his childhood.

This new cemetery, although imposing and grand, was too new to be frequented by phantoms, if they exist. And if they do, they would find no comfort here.

Such cemeteries are not haunted, of course; how could they be? Modern fields, where care is professional and permanent, have no gnarled trees to offer shade and rest for the gravediggers, and tombstones are upright and correct. There is little that resembles the small patches of land families set aside centuries ago in these hills for their dead and there is little to induce a reluctant shade to stay longer than its appointed time on earth.

In recent years, urban convention has arrived in the hills with corporate cemeteries offering relief for remaining family members from maintaining their old cemeteries, and fewer and fewer old mountain graveyards see new burials. But there is something missing now, as the old customs are rarely applied.

The Old Prater Cemetery was such a mountain burying-ground. It was younger than the small cemetery at the bottom of the hill where Hopkins first buried their dead, but after the Civil War, bottomland cemeteries became a luxury few families could afford. That first cemetery was too close to the precious narrow flat shelves of land between the mountains, the rich loam that was necessary for farming, for feeding the living, and it was ultimately closed.

It was also nearly obliterated by succeeding generations, and only a few stones remained. I knew practically nothing about that obscure place in the winter of 1997, except that Rissie knew who was buried there.

The first funeral on what would become the Old Prater Cemetery took place when there were no Praters on Greasy Creek to be buried. I did not know that for many years; I still did not know it when my father died. I actually knew little of the distant past, of what I speak of now so matter-of-factly. I had assumed the Old Prater was always a Prater cemetery, and the Hopkins were allowed to bury their dead in a steep corner because of the kindness of Peter Prater who was once its caretaker and was my great-grandfather on my mother's side. That lack of knowledge was a gap in my education, one I ignored for nearly fifty years, but which would close rapidly in the next five.

Over nearly a century and a half, the succeeding generations of the dead had consumed all of the flatter land the Old Prater could offer. All that was left was the steep hillside behind the cemetery, the place where Jim Prater, Peter's brother, planted corn, but it was too steep even for mountain cemeteries. I had walked there with my father many times after cleaning the cemetery for Decoration Day, just as our ancestors had done for generations. We would sit there and look over our work. The wind always seemed to pick up to cool us after wielding scythes or reap hooks through the previous year's weeds and brush. It was a place where we could review our work, as had all our ancestors, but it was an inescapable fact that the cemetery was filling up.

There were other reasons for my father's election of the Annie E. Young Cemetery as his final resting-place; perhaps he had been prescient. Greasy Creek was changing, and to the worse. Strip mining was devastating the land all over the coal fields, and Greasy Creek was one of the first victims. In the hollow behind the cemetery, a mine operated day and night, intruding into the tranquillity of the hollow the Old Prater guarded. But other hollows were not as fortunate: Joe Boner Hollow, just up the road and named incorrectly, perhaps scatologically, for a Revolutionary War soldier who came here with a land grant when it was still part of Virginia, was a prime example. Filled to its mouth with rock and dirt when the mountaintops were torn away for the thin seams of coal that lay beneath, even the lost grave of Joseph Bowney, North Carolina soldier in service to the new country, was covered. All for the hard compressed vegetation of another age, turned black over the eons, and dug to feed the boilers of utility companies.

It was only a matter of time before the entire length of Greasy Creek would become a moonscape, as dry and pockmarked as the ancient satellite that illuminated it. The hills would appear green when the rains came, but with the coarsest of plants, those that could endure the desert that strip mining left behind, pulling surface water with voracious roots, for there was no longer a water table for deeper thirsts.

Perhaps my father knew that, so he established a new tradition for his clan by moving to the Annie E. Young. He knew he would be the first of us to be buried there; his diabetes was taking its toll when he purchased the plots. He knew it was necessary to make that decision. In spite of the logic, it was not an easy choice.

For generations, the Hopkins and the Praters in my line were buried in the Old Prater. Over a hundred graves of both the Hopkins on my father's side and the Praters on my mother's were in repose, and it was a sacred chore to clean off the cemetery every year for Decoration Day. It was an annual reunion, as distant relatives came in from Ohio and other emigrant places in Buicks and Oldsmobiles and other fine cars with store-bought flowers to supplement the spooned crepe paper roses we carried. The week before the event, we would cut the weeds in the cemetery, clean the vegetation from the graves and rake the surrounding earth to mound them up again. It was an old mountain tradition to mound up the graves with new soil, making them appear like fresh scars that could be salved only by the flowers we would place on them.

A few years before my father died, we stopped mounding the graves. "I don't like to see them like that," he said. "It just makes it hurt all over again."

I felt the same way, but said nothing. After that, we let the graves settle into the earth.

I would never have to do these chores for my father's grave, and I felt a certain loss. I was thankful that he had the foresight to see that the old cemetery was too crowded and too isolated for the family to care for. In his usual way, he tried to make it as easy on his children as he could. But it would have been an honor to take care of his grave as long as I lived. My father would not be buried near his father, nor his mother, nor his grandfather, nor any other soul whose blood he shared, but I knew he was right in that decision. He knew that his sons would never neglect the graves of his ancestors. That must have comforted him when he selected another place for his own tomb.

The night after his funeral, I dreamed. Not the usual dream in which the mind seeks to make sense of some physical or psychic discomfort, but a dream from my childhood, a dream I had not dreamed in decades, but which returned with all the sharpness of the unclouded day in which we buried my father:

I am walking the crumbling streets of the old coal town where my grandmother lives. It is two miles from my home up the creek and I have come down on a hot August day to visit my grandmother who lives in what was once a company house. There are only a few of them remaining from the heyday of the mine, when every one of the identical, sturdy two-story buildings held two families living side by side. The houses were owned by the company, just as the miners themselves were. Rissie Prater's house sits alone in the largest lot in what is left of the town, but although alone, it is never lonely, for there are always people on the porches.

She is one of my three grandmothers, and always welcomes me with open arms. She has a broad smile, full of pride and love, and I step more lightly, as through the honeysuckle-covered fence, I see her sitting on the front porch where family and friends are sitting, escaping the late summer heat. I know that I bring joy to her when I visit, and I often walk off Gardner Fork to the old Greasy Creek camp where her house stands. She lives in the house she purchased with the insurance money from her husband's death—the final toll many paid to the Greasy Creek mine. Her gardens, which occupy the plots where houses once stood, are full of corn and beans and sweet potatoes and sunflowers. Beside the peeling house there are orange day lilies and pink roses, so pale and delicate they are nearly white.

Nothing remains of the other houses but the concrete bases of the chimneys that stand mute, as if they were the smooth faces of unfinished tombstones that stand guard over, and refuse to admit any information on their dead.

As I approach the gate, held shut by a metal weight on a rusted chain, I smell honeysuckle; I am nearly intoxicated from its scent, heavy and pungent in the still air and my nostrils flare as I pull in every particle of its lushness. I open the gate and begin to walk toward the porch. I know my grandmother will get up from her chair to embrace me and kiss me on the forehead, and introduce me to those people. I will try to be a good boy and listen to them speak. They will talk about my

15

family, about those who have gone before, and I will listen and forget, unless my father's name is mentioned, for I am a child and such things are of little interest to me.

But when the gate closes, and I look around, I am no longer on the company-built sidewalk to my grandmother's house. Instead, I am on the twisted upland path into the Old Prater Cemetery. There is still the overpowering scent of honeysuckle, but it is from the rusted fence surrounding the graveyard. Instead of sunflowers drooping in my grandmother's garden, I see the tilted headstones of the dead. This is curious, I think; I am alone in a cemetery, a place of ghost stories and Halloween revelries, but I am not afraid. But I have never been afraid here; there is always a sweetness about this place that elicits no fear, a placidity that somehow offers me peace.

Ahead of me, in the shadow of the trees overhanging my great-grandfather's grave, is another gathering. Their apparel is not what I am accustomed to, and the men, unlike my father, are not clean-shaven and the women, some sitting, some standing, fidget nervously at my approach. I know they are family for I see my father in their faces, but I have never touched them, I have never seen them breathe or heard them speak, but I know they are my blood. They are smiling, without guile, and they wait for me, as I shamble toward them at my childish pace. There are men and women and children, and I know I will be welcome there, and I smile back.

This time it will be no chore to listen. Their faces are becoming clearer and I know they will tell me things that are important, things I should know, and I quicken my step.

But I never arrive; as it always has, the dream ends before I join their circle, and darkness sweeps over me until I awaken.

I had always assumed the dream was merely some electro-chemical reaction: a way my brain established my mortality; I too would join the ghosts of the cemetery when it was my time. There would have to be a logical explanation, the way doctors explain away near-death experiences to their patients. It was all some arcane biochemistry, a palliative, a shot of endorphins the body gives itself to lessen the pain of death.

16

WINTER

That was all it could be, I thought.

The dream visited me often when I was a child at Middle Greasy Grade School, when after every death in the family, I could look from the playground to the Old Prater up on the hill and see the fresh grave in the distance. But the dream came less frequently after I went to high school, and it disappeared from my memory as I struggled through the Sixties with the other Boomers of my generation. There were realities and alternative realities enough for everyone during those times; I needed no adolescent fantasies to compete for my consciousness, so I had nearly forgotten it by the time I became an adult.

But it came back unexpectedly the winter night when my father called me in Virginia to tell me my grandfather Frank had died. In succeeding years, each time someone in the family would pass away, it would come again, and each time I would dismiss those visitations as part of the grieving process.

Mere synaptic activity looking for a circuit, I thought. A way for my subconscious to compensate for a loss, that's all it is.

And I had nearly forgotten the dream until the night after my father's funeral.

Perhaps it never visited me at all; perhaps I merely summoned it each of those times, to gain some comfort from the past, to recapture what it felt like to be a child again and surrounded by goodness. But it came to me that winter, and I know it did not attend me at my bidding.

In the spring following my father's death, a newspaper story appeared about a public meeting sponsored by the Kentucky Department of Transportation on the reconstruction of U.S. Highway 460. I decided to go just to see if the rumors were true that it would come through Greasy Creek. Only my mother and my brother still lived there; my home was a half-hour's drive away and my sister lived in Tennessee. Since my mother lived alone, I had misgivings about what disruptions the road might cause her. Except for the time she riveted wings on B-24's in Michigan during the war and except for the one year our family lived in Ohio, my mother had spent her entire life on

17

Greasy Creek. I feared for her well being if her house fell victim to the roadway.

But there were some possible benefits. My brother had purchased my Prater grandparents' crumbling old house to convert into apartments. It was near the proposed roadway and might be taken by construction. I thought it would be a blessing to him to have the KYDOT absorb that unproductive venture. The Prater house was a long block structure that once housed a store as well as living quarters, but my grandfather Andrew had not used the best materials to build it and my brother had far more expense than he anticipated in its conversion. The money he got from rent rarely covered the damage done by the renters when they drank and fought and skipped out, ignoring the broken doors and windows and usually the unpaid utilities.

Maybe some good could come from this after all, I thought.

There was little else of importance the construction would touch, I determined. Rissie's house in the Greasy Creek camps had been torn down a decade before. There was the possibility that construction might take her solitary grave and allow me to return her to the Old Prater to rest beside Harlen Damron, her first husband, and one of my father's two fathers.

Before she died in 1979, Rissie surprised us all when she said she would not be buried on the Old Prater. Neither would Perry Prater, her second husband, be buried beside his first wife. Instead, they would both be buried on the hillside overlooking her house. But Perry's last wife would not bury him beside Rissie, so she slept alone. My father had long wanted to move her to the Old Prater so she would be near Harlen forever, and the couple who raised him would be together again.

But Rissie was not really my grandmother, and she was neither a Damron nor a Prater; those were her married names. She was born Rissie Hopkins, a younger sister to my grandfather Frank Hopkins. She was also born with a cleft palate; an occasional deformity visited upon the Hopkins, and a clubfoot, probably from polio in the womb before she was born. Her cleft palate and attendant harelip was corrected when she was young, after surgery for such things became common, unlike her father, Harrison, who also had a harelip that was never closed. He was born a year after the Civil War ended and he went to his grave in 1937 with great mustaches to hide the disfigurement there was no way to correct or money with which it could be corrected.

I knew little about Harrison's life and his times, except that it was difficult to make a living off the crowded farmland of Greasy Creek; Rissie told me so. She told me many stories while lifting her hand to her mouth to hide her scar.

The line on her upper lip was a reminder of a deformity, just as one of her shoes would always be twisted and worn when the other was still serviceable, but because of her beauty, I never saw these things. Neither did anyone else who ever knew her. She was one of those people who always had a glow, some astral light that blinded us to anything that could have been wrong with her on an earthly scale.

Rissie was not yet nineteen when Ethel died. Manie Ethel Coleman Hopkins was my paternal grandmother and she died before my father could develop a memory of the woman who bore him. Her death was nearly as devastating to Rissie as it was for her brother Frank, who had married Ethel after he returned from the battlefields of France. Rissie had buried her mother, become housekeeper for her father, and watched her brother collapse under the strain of watching most of his family die in his arms.

After the Great War, Frank and his brother Bud returned to the quiet hills of Kentucky which they both had thought they would never see again as they sat in the trenches of France waiting for the shells to drop. When the sirens sounded or the whistles blew, they would frantically push on the gas masks that were supposed to keep them safe. But when the hated green cloud swept over them, burning their skins as they strained to breathe through the heavy canisters, they were not always successful and both of them carried scarred lungs from mustard gas to the grave.

Things were returning to normal in late fall of 1918, when the war was drawing to a close, and a new prosperity had swept into the hills. Mines were opening and there was plenty of work for the boys who would soon return. The first wave of Spanish Influenza had passed when Frank got home, and he wasted no time in courting Ethel, who had lush black hair and creamy white skin. When they married, the new couple moved in with Harrison for a while, just until Frank could build their own house for Ethel and their baby. They named him Warren G for President Warren G. Harding, a good Republican name, and had another they named Marion, for Frank's grandfather.

But their idyll soon ended.

Spanish Influenza had spread through the hills of eastern Kentucky in the winter of 1918-19 and Frank's mother was among the victims. He saw more death when he came back form the war than he saw in the horrific fields of France. The sheer number of deaths from the flu had been so staggering that the Kentucky Legislature forbade public funerals, and the locations of many graves were lost forever when the gravediggers themselves died without revealing or marking their work. For years afterward, death returned to pick up those who had survived the first wave, but who had become so weakened that they could not fight off pneumonia or tuberculosis when the weather closed them in.

Ethel had sickened in the first wave, but survived and did not trouble Frank with the news. Frank took her to Huntington, West Virginia when she sickened again, and the doctors took out a rib, but could not cure her. The loss of her first son when the flu returned was the final straw. She died soon afterward. Frank had not fully recovered from the war and had no more resources to call upon when he found his other son wheezing and near death himself.

His own mother had died only a few years before and his father, heartbroken, became a stranger in his own house. How could Frank take care of his shattered father and his young sisters and contend with a child that would surely die soon? He asked Ethel's parents to take the child until he could sort out his own life.

Paris Roscoe Coleman was the grandson of David Coleman who had fought in the Civil War. His wife Pernina Damron was the daughter of Robert Damron who had fought alongside Dave in the same regiment. As a child, she had tended her parents and then tended her own children and she knew how to raise a child. Paris and Nina knew how to face adversity in the poverty of post-Civil War Eastern Kentucky and had taught Ethel well. It was a good choice, and Rissie went over to Paris and Nina's every day to visit her nephew. But not long afterward, a bitter confrontation broke out between two of Paris' brothers, or more correctly, between a brother and another brother's wife and the latter shot the former dead. Graveyard-dead, one of my relatives once told me, as if to emphasize that her bullet went straight through his heart.

Afterward, the remaining Colemans chose up sides and Paris decided to leave Greasy Creek so he would not have to take one brother's side over the other. He told Frank they were leaving, and they would come for the baby, who was staying with Rissie while the Colemans battled. But Frank changed his mind; he would not give up his child. His mother, his wife, and his first son had all died in front of him. If Marion were to die, it would be here on Greasy and not in some far-away place where his wasted body would have no comfort and where no familiar spirits would be there to welcome him to his rest.

Almost as an afterthought, he turned to his sister, who was bursting with hope that the child would be hers. Her heart nearly leaped out of her chest when he asked her; it was what she was hoping for from the depths of her being.

"Rissie, you're going to have to take the baby for me," he said. "He's sick and I don't know what to do."

Rissie had loved her brother Frank and his wife Ethel and she had loved their two children more than she loved anything else in her life. Because of her malformations, she expected no marriage, no family of her own, and she had transferred to her brother all hopes for everything she knew she would never have. When Frank's family disintegrated, she thought she would go mad herself.

But that had passed. The sum of all her dreams was lying in front of her, feverish and dysenteric and barely breathing. She had no time for self-pity or equivocation; she had a job to do and she was determined to succeed.

Marion was now her child, and she used all her power to save his life. She no longer called him Marion; she had seen that name on too many tombstones; his name would now be Marvin. She consulted the old women of the creek for their remedies. They scarified him, making a small cut in his back and mixing the blood with milk in his bottle for him to drink, but it did not help. She took him to a child who had never seen its father, who could therefore heal the sick, and had it breathe into Marvin's mouth, but he weakened more. When those remedies failed, she took him to the company doctor, but he told her there was nothing he could do: the child would soon die.

Finally, she used her own instincts, and reset the terms of her battle. She stayed up, night after night, cooling his inflamed body with well water and alcohol, and would not sleep until he rested. She sang to him, songs her grandmother had sung to her, until the fight went out of him and his fever broke.

Eventually, he began to sleep and eat, and she knew he would live. She nursed him back to health, and fell more in love with him every day, as he grew stronger and gained weight.

Not only was there a change in her child, there was a change in her as well. The glow that I always saw in her, the aura that overwhelmed all her infirmities soon became apparent to everyone.

Something happened to Rissie when she saved her son; she lost the unsteady gait her twisted foot had caused and she walked upright and proud with no hesitation. It was not merely that people now ignored her clubfoot, it was as if it had never existed and all its hurtful memory had been erased. Her smiles, furtive at best to minimize the wound to her upper lip, became wide and full of pride and promise and the blue-gray eyes she shared with her son lit up when people asked her about him. Her stories of Marvin and his growing up became the delight of everyone who knew her. As a young mother, she became more beautiful than any young girl on Greasy Creek, even if she did not have their symmetrical lips and graceful feet.

The boys began to recognize her as well. Those who had laughed at her or teased her fell silent when she walked by. "Is that Rissie Hopkins?" they asked. Something drew them to her, but nothing drew her to them. She was happy now; happier than she had ever been and she ignored them, paying no attention to the crestfallen swains who once mocked her in their youthful stupidity. But there was one boy who never mocked her, and she could not deny her attraction for him.

When she fell in love with Harlen Damron, the handsomest men on the creek, he was already in love with her. He asked her to marry him, but she said she would not if he did not accept Marvin as their son, but by that time there was no reason to make a demand. He had fallen in love with the frail child who had Rissie's eyes, and he became their first child, although he was not the issue of either of them. They soon had another, a daughter they named Bobbie Jean.

By then, Frank had pieced together his life and he came for his boy. He had married again and had a daughter he named Ima Jean, but Rissie, forever now Marvin's mother, refused to give him up.

"Frank, we've raised him and he's our son too," she said. "You can't have him back for all time, but if he wants to stay with you some he can do that. But he's mine, you gave him to me."

Frank had no choice but to agree and accepted the arrangement Rissie offered him. Thus, my father grew up with two families and two sisters. Consequently, when Marvin married Pansy and I came along, I grew up with three sets of grandparents and for years I thought everyone did. One set did not include Harlen, however.

He died in 1940, six years before I was born, from pneumonia after his skull was crushed by a rock-fall while junking the old Greasy Creek mine. Rissie buried him on the steep upper edge of the Old Prater, where her father's family was buried, and reserved a spot for herself at his feet.

With the insurance money from Harlen's death, Rissie bought a house for her and Bobbie Jean from the coal company that was selling off the last of its assets on Greasy Creek. The house Harlen had built for her in Snake Branch, just above Harrison's house on Gardner Fork, had too many memories and she sold it to Frank and Laura, his wife.

Eventually, Rissie married again, to Peter Prater's widowed nephew Perry. He was only the second Prater to marry a Hopkins, and I often wondered why the Hopkins and Praters were buried together but never lived together. My father and my mother was the first such union, and it produced three children. Rissie and Perry were the second, but it was a twilight marriage for them both and they had no children. Perry, although older, outlived Rissie by twenty years and married again. That was a post-twilight marriage for him, but it was not as happy. How could it be? Who could ever replace Rissie Hopkins?

I drove by Rissie's old place on the way to the meeting, but I saw few reminders of what it was like growing up there. The old house had been torn down, and a young couple now very happily lived there in a new house built on the spot. The place was clean, and there was nothing to give me pause. The honeysuckle was gone, as was the old rusted fence, now replaced by modern chain-link. There were, in fact, few reminders of the town that once surrounded my grandmother's house. Except for the decaying Greasy Creek Hotel, there was nothing from the porch of the new house that corresponded to the view I grew up with. But it didn't matter; I no longer lived on Greasy Creek and cared little about its fate.

There was a large crowd at Shelby Valley High School when I arrived. There were large maps, aerial photographs, and representatives of the Kentucky Department of Transportation available to answer questions and explain the processes involved. The crowd, mostly from Greasy Creek, was mostly interested in how they would be paid for giving up their land. A team of appraisers, they were told, would make an offer based on market value.

Maybe my brother could unload his apartments, I thought. Get him out of debt, at least, on his money pit.

There was other information: any cemeteries to be moved would be done at public expense; an off-ramp would be built into Greasy Creek, allowing that ancient place to have access to this most modern road in Pike County when it was completed. The Greasy Creek road would be upgraded to handle new traffic to the on-ramp. All this was good news, as I desultorily moved from exhibit to exhibit.

But I froze as I looked at the aerial photographs and the route overlays that showed where construction would take place: *the road would take the hollow behind my parents' house. Snake Branch would no longer exist. The cove where I grew up, and its hillsides where I killed my first and only raccoon and swore never to kill another animal, would be filled with rock a hundred feet high. The place where I stole a cigarette and smoked it in emulation of my cousin Caudill, and fell through the barn floor in divine punishment for my sin, would be gone. The house were Rissie and Harlen lived, where Frank and Laura lived, where the teenagers of Greasy Creek gathered on Saturday nights before World War II would be gone.*

How could they do that? Was there no other route?

My parent's house would not be taken, and I was grateful, but there would be no more Snake Branch.

But that discovery was not as devastating as the next one. A closer look at the schematic overlays revealed something even more sinister: *the Old Prater Cemetery was directly in line of the new road.*

Christ, I thought, this can't be.

The cemetery was sacred; the graveyard, with its leaning stones and irregular pathways, was the one place on Greasy

Creek that had to be held inviolate. The very essence of my family was buried there. Amid the strip mines, the poverty, and the ugly pollution of its streams, would the only beautiful thing to me on Greasy Creek now be lost as well?

For a long time I stood there, attempting to assimilate the horror of what I knew was coming, but I had always fancied myself the pragmatist. After alternating flashes of fear, anger, and then grief, I settled on rationalization. If the cemetery were moved, I realized I wouldn't have to go through the agonizing job of cleaning it and decorating the graves every year. I flushed with shame for thinking that, but then remembered my father's logic: at least the graves would be in a convenient place for the family. After all, hadn't Pop decided to be buried on the Annie E. Young to spare us from the burden of maintaining his grave?

When they told me the reinterment site was that same cemetery, I was profoundly relieved. My father's gravesite would not be bereft of kin after all, and my rationalization no longer seemed so selfish.

Although my childhood playground would be lost, along with the cemetery, something good would have to come of this. I began making plans for moving my family graves.

I called Bobbie Jean in Ohio to see if she wanted me to take Rissie up to be buried beside Harlen when the other graves were reinterred. She agreed and I contacted the KYDOT to make the arrangements and the new cemetery sales office to secure Rissie's place beside the man she loved.

So be it, I thought.

I assumed that was all I could do. Except for whatever minor details my brother and I would have to attend to for our family graves, my intervention in this matter was over.

As an afterthought, I wondered if the state highway department would be able to identify all the graves in the Old Prater, but gave it little additional consideration.

I had other things to deal with.

My job was becoming nightmarish. The school system, for which I was the very visible spokesman, had become plagued with criminal investigations. After a bitter year of divisiveness and recriminations among the school board and the staff of the school system, the superintendent resigned, and I took a mundane job overseeing the insurance program. I collapsed into bed every night exhausted from the stress of merely going to work and I was thankful I had no other responsibilities.

But soon I did.

There was a price to pay for absolving me of my promise to take care of the Old Prater. The KYDOT would make no effort to identify the unknown graves on cemeteries to be moved, relying on family members to supply that information. If there were no one to make that identification, the graves would be moved and marked "unknown." I thought that grossly unfair, and my brother and I began to talk to family members about the graves.

My brother was Public Health Director for the county and was a dedicated public servant. Unusual in a place where political machines controlled most of the public jobs, an honest Board of Health had selected him and he was devoted to his work. Promoting public health required much of his free time, speaking to groups and participating in campaigns for better sewers or cleaner water or fighting against smoking or any of the other dangers of living in Pike County, Kentucky. Consequently, he had little time to pursue family history.

By contrast, I had quite a bit of time on my hands after my superintendent's fall, since my job was very low profile, as the new administration wanted. I was no longer the spokesman for the school system, and did not want to be. Most importantly, I now had nights and weekends to myself.

The research on the cemetery had to be done. I did not know where this minor genealogical research would lead, but I began making the rounds of my living relatives for information.

I began this work with reluctance and some resentment. Why could no one else do this, I wondered? Is there no one left who can tell me whom these odd rocks and mounds of earth represent? Where are the elders of the family who knew all the stories of the Old Prater?

Duh, I thought, they're buried here.

With no recourse but to do the work, I began seriously researching the past.

And I began to see things: not immediately, and at first not consciously.

Something happened as my research intensified: from bits and pieces of family history, from my own faded recollections, I began to see images, and remember voices that I had not heard in decades.

From fragments of stories my grandmother told me in childhood, I began to reconstruct another world, one far-removed from the squalor of present-day Greasy Creek. It seemed almost to build itself, and began to emerge, Brigadoon-like, in the mists as I trudged up the twisted road to where my ancestors lay.

Perhaps I knew, somewhere deep inside, that someday I would have had to take on this job. Perhaps I knew that I would ultimately bury everyone I loved, and that whatever bad karma I had engendered from my dissolute youth would return to exact its price. Maybe I had been warned, but I had been too reckless to care, or too resentful.

And then I realized I had been warned, many years before.

Just before Decoration Day in 1955, family began to gather, as usual, at our house. It was the annual chore: the men of the family would collect their tools and go up to the Old Prater and other family cemeteries to clean off the graves. As the men were working, the women would spoon brightly colored crepe paper into shapes of roses and tulips and when finished with their respective duties, they would all adjourn to the cemeteries to decorate the graves.

A few weeks before, my father had gone to Ohio to find work, along with a dozen other men of Greasy Creek who left when the coal mines closed on one of their usual down cycles. He had come home after driving all night following his evening shift stamping fenders for new Fords in Cleveland, and was ready to decorate the graves at first light. My mother made him sleep for a few hours instead. My brother and my sister and I paced the living room, waiting for him to wake up. When he did, we got our hugs and had breakfast together. It seemed like he had never been gone, and I would not think about Monday morning without him.

With the grandparents and our boxes of homemade flowers, we went up to the cemetery. It was to be a fateful day. I knew something about the graves and had begun to make associations, but as we worked that day, I realized I knew nothing of Harrison's ancestors.

"Where is Grandpaw Harrison's daddy buried?" I asked my grandfather Frank. He said nothing, as he and my grandmother Laura, his second wife, continued to push artificial flowers into the ground. I got no response from Rissie either. My mother said nothing. *Something is wrong here, I thought.* I knew my father had also heard my question, but he avoided my eyes when I searched for an answer. Finally, he spoke.

"We don't know who his father was," he said. "He took his mother's name." He took his mother's name? I was old enough to know what that meant. My great-grandfather was illegitimate. He was a bastard! I had heard the term, and I knew what it meant. I had heard the jokes and the deprecations leveled against bastards on the creek, and I was humiliated.

Could it be your own fault if you were a bastard?

"Was he a good man?" I asked my father.

"He was a real good man," my father replied, surprised at the question.

I was relieved.

"He was a real good man," Rissie echoed. But it was not enough for me. When we finished our work my cheeks were red with shame and I would never look at the cemetery the same way again. I wanted to avoid what it now meant to me.

I accepted, or ignored, my great-grandfather's bastardy when I grew up, but I no longer had the interest in family history I had when I was very young and Rissie would put me to sleep at night with her stories. Now I had no link to any Hopkins before Harrison, who wasn't really a Hopkins at all. There were no ancient family heroes, I decided, who would be worth learning about; my father, my grandfather, and my great-grandfather were enough.

I had heard talk occasionally of a "Lige Hopkins," who was supposedly Harrison's grandfather, and a scandalous person, but since I was not really a Hopkins, what did it matter? I decided then that no one past Harrison was worth finding, and for decades, family history meant nothing to me. I began to lose the stories my grandmother had filled my mind with when I was a child.

In the spring after my father died, I climbed the hill again for Decoration Day. I had cleaned it earlier and I was helping a widowed aunt decorate the graves. She was Ola Robinson Prater, widow of Avery Prater, my mother's older brother. We started with Harrison's and went on up the Hopkins section, for Ola was Harrison's granddaughter as well. Her mother Alice was buried above my grandfather Frank. To the left of Frank's grave was Ethel's and the infant Warren G's, and to the right of my grandfather's grave was the grave of Harrison Hopkins, Jr., another infant, who was the first child of Frank and Laura. (She was buried above him, beside her own mother, as there was no room in Frank's plot.) Laura and Frank had lost their first child, whom they named after Harrison, just as Ethel and Frank had lost their first son. I could understand why my father was a much happier man than my grandfather.

On the hillsides of Greasy Creek on Decoration Day, it is yet a young time of year, and I could see a few fading spring flowers, jonquils and crocuses, still blooming among the graves. The honeysuckle had not yet taken over the fence, but I detected a faint air of it as I helped my aunt place store-bought flowers on the graves. There were so many graves, and the earth that harbored them was claiming them, little by little. I remarked to my aunt that someone ought to write down who was buried here, so that their places would not be forgotten. I did not say the obvious: that since both she and I were childless, there would be no other generation to care for these old graves.

I did not know this would not be my last trip to the cemetery until next Decoration Day and that I would be returning often over the next five years. But I could sense, somehow, I had more work to do here—work beyond merely cleaning off and decorating graves.

There were words that were echoing in my mind in the bright spring sunlight of that May afternoon, words from an odd passage I once happened upon in Rissie's Bible, words that were resonating like a grandfather clock, repeating themselves in my mind. Amid the graves of my ancestors, with honeysuckle wafting in the air, and with the memory of the dream I had—and would have again—of this place, I could hear the ancient admonition: *Remove not the ancient landmark, which thy fathers have set.*

A Greasy Creek Anthology

"Seventy-two graves?" I asked the Kentucky Department of Transportation representative. "That's all? I thought there'd be more."

"There might be," he replied. "These are the graves the engineers found, including about twenty unknowns."

I disagree, I thought. There are more than twenty.

"Much of the cemetery is obscured by weeds," he said.

That I agreed with. It was a chore to clean it off, or even get to it since the old road was covered by debris from the KYDOT's exploration of the site. But it had never been easy. I had not realized how difficult it was to go there in my youth; perhaps I simply had more energy or fewer reasons not to go. Perhaps it was merely the fact that visiting the cemetery was a family affair then, and there were crowds of faces, even if I knew only a few of them. Now I could barely find time to do the work.

Perhaps the riotous undergrowth had something to do with global warming. The coal ripped from the mountains of Greasy Creek had fueled the factories and power plants that helped to develop the nation, and may also have contributed to heating up the world. The weeds on the Old Prater seemed to have grown exponentially every year and the summers seemed hotter. Whatever the case, it would be much easier to visit the graves at the Annie E. Young Cemetery, and they would be tended perpetually.

"If you think there are other graves, I can arrange for the engineers to meet you there sometime for further exploration," he said, reverting a little to bureau-speak. He was cognizant of the sensitivity of the issue.

"Oh, there are others in there, somewhere in all that mess," I said. "Right now, I don't know where. Let me see what I can find and I'll get back to you. By the way, what's the procedure for getting a forensic anthropologist to help me identify the unknown graves?"

"A forensic anthropologist? I don't know," he said, apparently surprised. "We've never had a request for one before."

"Well, I'll need one. Some of these unknown graves are probably a hundred years old."

"I'll check into it," he said, and extended his hand, which I took. I picked up the map and left. It was time to go up the hill one more time to the Old Prater.

It was late fall and the cemetery was again overrun and ready for its biannual sprucing-up.. The cleaning we had given it in spring had yielded to a summer of unfettered growth and, except for the Hopkins family graves, the cemetery was nearly covered by the dying grass and weeds. It was a custom of the family to gather at the foot of the hill twice each year, once for Decoration Day or as it is more commonly called now, Memorial Day, and again for Labor Day for a family reunion for the descendants of Harrison Hopkins. Family members, Hopkinses and Robinsons, came in from Akron or Louisville, or other cities where the family had migrated.

In the 1970's there were great crowds at these gatherings. But every year, as more of the elders died off, fewer people came back, and even though we regularly cleaned off all the Hopkins graves and many of the Praters, people rarely visited anymore. The Robinsons tended their own family cemetery nearby, and still had church services there, but the Old Prater had been a lonely place for years.

There was something else to these annual affairs, something rarely talked about, and something that did not interest me when it was brought up at odd times in the past. Apparently, the Hopkinses and Robinsons shared a single ancestor: Elisha Hopkins, "Ol' Lige," as Rissie called him.

My cousin Caudill once said that he tried to do his family tree, but when it ended up in illegitimacy on either side, he said the hell with it. What I did not know then was that both the Hopkins and the Robinsons descended from cantankerous, foul-mouthed, whore-hopping Ol' Lige, apparently my great-great-great grandfather who had five or six wives and fifty children, or so the stories went. Typical for Greasy Creek, I thought. Just something else about my past I wanted no part of.

I eagerly listened to the stories about Harrison, but I had no desire to know anything of Lige, whom Rissie would threaten recalcitrant children with association for their behavior. But mostly we talked about the people buried in the Old Prater, where Lige was not buried, I knew. And every year fewer and fewer people would make the upland trek to the cemetery.

My sister had assumed the burden of making sure the graves were decorated as the women of the family died off, and when Dad was alive she would come home from Tennessee to perform that task. My father would clean the cemetery and my sister would place flowers in front of the stones. They decorated the marked graves as well as the few lonely stones that neither bore a name nor had family attend them. But modern life permits little time for the old ways and as the elders passed, so did the traditions. As long as Dad was alive he would make sure the cemetery was presentable, but with his death, the last of the caretakers was gone. Only one other Hopkins branch found the time to scrape and decorate their graves for Memorial Day and, in fact, still mounded them, but there were no others by the time my father died. Sadly, most of the Prater graves were rarely even mowed.

It was a far cry from the early days of my memory, when all the families would venture to the graveyard and share food and stories as the graves reappeared out of the undergrowth. It was a true family reunion then, and the cemetery seemed more like a friendly garden where neighbors chatted over fences than a place of mourning. If ghosts were watching, they would have been like grandmothers, beaming at their progeny playing in the lanes between the graves. Now it was a struggle for me to find the time to cut the sedge and poke that grew wildly on that fertile plot.

My sister kept most of the information on the past. Joanetta Hopkins Spears Cassie, MD, still known as "Bug" to the family and to her eternal consternation, became the family historian after Rissie died, and I assumed that would always be her lot. She was brilliant and had a tremendous memory that served her well in medical school. By contrast, I hated the though of remembering things that meant nothing to me and I suffered from forgetting names, a genetic trait inherited from my father, who forgot names, sometimes even his children's. My father's predilection for substituting "whatchacallit" for memory lapses was the source of many stories about him, and he thoroughly enjoyed them all.

I learned to overcome that gene somewhat as my work progressed; and was able to rattle off new information even weeks after I learned it, but maybe I was merely *relearning* it. I suspect that knowledge was always there, but there was no chemical link to connect it to anything I considered important. Now when old names appeared in a new context, an odd vibration ensued. Faces from my old dream about the cemetery began slowly to come into focus.

While I was at the KYDOT office, we spoke briefly of the other cemetery to be moved. I knew there was another cemetery on the way to the Old Prater, but there was no plat for me. That was no problem; the few graves in that cemetery could be seen in their entirety in one glance. In fact, there was not much left of it, just a few stones, and I knew nothing of who was buried there, other than they were in the Hopkins family. I knew that much because I remembered the sheer fury I observed, for the only time in my life, in Rissie's eyes.

It was sometime in the 1950's, during one of the annual Memorial Day pilgrimages, or "Decoration Day" as it was called then on Greasy Creek, when the family exited their vehicles and was allotting supplies to various members according to their ages and strength that I heard my grand-mother exchanging some heated words with Jim Prater, who owned the land on which both cemeteries sat. I was to carry two boxes of paper flowers the women had made and was waiting for my grandmother in case she needed help climbing the hill. I could see her, standing erect and defiant, shaking her finger at Jim and pointing to the cemetery, her hands waving as she spoke.

Jim was my great-great uncle, a younger brother of my great-grandfather Peter Prater, who was known as Paw Pete to everyone on the creek, regardless of whether they were related. It was a term of respect for one of Greasy Creek's oldest citizens and one of its most alert, in spite of his age. Until he died at 101, he was still quite mobile and very much acute to the world around him. He spoke regularly on the telephone, and had more than one female friend to count among his correspondents. Apparently, sexual attraction, for or to the opposite sex, was not an exclusive Hopkins trait as I had thought when I was told about Jessie and Pearl.

But I never saw Jim at Peter's house, while his other living brothers or sisters would be there often. Nor did I ever see Peter at Jim's. It seemed somewhat unusual to me, and I knew that Jim often disagreed with his brothers and sisters over cemetery affairs, and perhaps that was the reason the Praters finally gave up tending their part of the cemetery.

On this occasion, however, my tiny, crippled grandmother was bearding the lion in his den, and I had never seen my grandmother so inflamed. My mother and I were standing near a hog pen that had been recently erected, just beside the path to the Old Prater, as we waited for Rissie and Jim to finish their conversation. My father had already gone up the hill, taking the hoes and mowing scythes to begin the task of cleaning the cemetery. I was confused about all this, for I had never seen my grandmother angry before. She had always been the epitome of quiet patience.

"What's wrong with Mamaw?" I asked my mother.

"She's mad at Jim," my mother replied.

"What about?"

"This hog pen," she said, looking at the fenced-in area where three or four snorting brown and black animals were rooting in the oozing, foul mire of the pen. *She doesn't want Jim to raise hogs, I wondered? Everybody raises hogs.*

"There's a cemetery in there," my mother said.

My eyes widened. *A cemetery? How could anyone build a hog pen over a cemetery? Who would do such a thing?*

At that time, as if to punctuate my horror, one of the hogs released a leisurely yellow stream into the ground. I could not comprehend such an affront to the dead.

"Who's buried there?" I asked my mother.

"I don't know," she said. "Some Hopkinses is all I know."

My grandmother returned from her conversation with Jim, still fuming. She grumbled all the way up to the Old Prater. Her anger abated only slightly by the time we had finished decorating the graves, and when we came back down the hill, Jim was nowhere to be found.

"He'll move those hogs off there," my father said, grinning. "Or Mamaw will take a rolling pin to his head."

I had no doubt of that. My grandmother was one of the most protective people I ever knew, especially when it came to her children or her grandchildren. I saw then her sense of guardianship extended to the dead in her family as well. I wanted to ask her who was buried there, but I did not. I suspect I did not want to attach a name to graves covered by the excrement of hogs. And now I regretted not asking.

I had been told by the KYDOT that the small cemetery, which I knew had to be much older, was simply too small to qualify for the help I needed on the Old Prater. That was unfair, I thought, but policies were policies, and that's what they told me was the policy. And after all, the cemetery had once served as Jim Prater's hog pen, so perhaps that chapter in its existence had driven out all sanctity, along with any possibility of finding any information among its sunken stones.

Hogs defiling graves, I thought. It reminds me of what I read about Shiloh, when the soldiers that survived the day watched hogs feasting on entrails of the dead in the lightning flashes of the rainstorm that came the night after the battle. Decades later, it still made me shiver.

Although Jim lost that battle to Rissie, he won another with a nearby Primitive Baptist church. The Primitives, Hardshells as they were called on Greasy Creek, were once part of the Regular Baptist Church formed in 1871, as I learned in my research. The original church split around 1895 over the doctrinal issue of free will, with the new *Old* Regular Baptists and the new Primitive Baptists going their separate ways. The Old Regulars claimed direct lineage and continued having summer services on the Old Prater Cemetery. The Primitives, led by Harmon Robinson, who now lay in his own cemetery near the Old Prater, built a new church in the field near the school and began to hold church services there.

Jim had a general disdain for both, was never pleased that he was required to listen to their singing on their two-day weekend rituals. With the aid of a shrieking corn-grinding mill, he managed to drown out the most vocal members of the congregation when they began to sing. When the church complained to him, he said he just didn't have time to get all his corn ground during the week. The congregation determined they were fighting a losing battle, and eventually the churchhouse was abandoned. Its building was dismantled when the consolidated Greasy Creek Elementary School was built. It did not seem so long ago, but it had been nearly forty years.

I had to take an indirect route to the Old Prater, since the original path had been blocked by fallen trees and earth pushed into it to build temporary roads for the KYDOT to drill for core samples of the mountain. It did not occur to me when I saw the drilling rigs the year before that the assessment of the roadway obstacles might ultimately include the question of what to do with the Old Prater.

The new road to the cemetery was longer but not as steep, although it still required a Jeep for the final leg. *It would have been nice to have this road in the old days, I thought, considering the difficulty we had bringing coffins up the old path.* I wondered if there ever was another way up the hill so that hearses or carts might have been able to go all the way to the gate. And how long had people been coming to the cemetery, I wondered? To me, the Old Prater Cemetery was eternal; it simply had always been there, like the stars.

Directly across a small hollow from the road was the Harmon Robinson Cemetery, where Harmon and many of his descendants were buried. Most of his family lived in Akron, but every year they would return to the campsite at the bottom of the hill in their RV's and build fires to sit around at night and talk of the past. Actually, they would return twice, once for Memorial Day and again for Labor Day. The Diasporic Hopkins from other places would also gather and we would have a Hopkins/Robinson Family reunion, although the true common ancestor of our families was not buried in any of the three cemeteries nearby.

Elisha Hopkins was the central figure of our progeny and was buried high up on Ripley Knob, which overlooked our campground. Elisha was Harmon's father, but without benefit of marriage, so Harmon took his mother's surname. Harmon's cemetery was smaller, and much better maintained than the other two. I had recently revisited it to make a small plat. It would help me in the research I was going to do on the Old Prater. A thought occurred to me that the reason it was so well cared for was that it was a nuclear cemetery for the Robinsons, and because it was restricted to Harmon's descendants. Perhaps, I thought, if there were only Praters or Hopkins, instead of both on the Old Prater, it would have had better care.

And who knew who was buried on the small cemetery at the foot of the hill where Jim Prater's hogs once wallowed? After the Hog Pen Incident, I never walked by the plot without feeling an enervating sadness, a need to apologize to those lost souls, although I had nothing to do with Jim's desecration.

When I platted Harmon's cemetery, I found a few unknown graves, but these appeared to be infants, and not likely the grave of Sally Robinson, Harmon's mother. I had asked the Robinsons about Sally, but no one knew where she was buried. I was interested in her because her name kept cropping up in my research, along with Elisha's other women. The thought crossed my mind that Elisha might not have been too severe with his daughter Dorcus, who was my great-grandmother, for her illegitimate children. She had Harrison and then another named Joseph, but Elisha had many illegitimate children, including Harmon, and in fact had four families, two that were legal and two unconsecrated. But even with all his wives and children, he did not have the harems of his legend. And how could I judge him anyway? I wondered if the wilderness, the freedom of a wild country away from the established churches of the East, give rise to such behavior, for there were other pioneers with many descendants. I wondered: can morals exist only where there are the comfortable trappings of civilization?

But ethics and philosophy were not part of my research, so I turned again to my work.

The Old Prater was on an slightly elevated flat behind a tiny meadow on the hillside. The meadow was formed by nature, but a further elevation of the lower part of the cemetery was formed by the debris collected by a century of fences placed there to keep out the cattle that once grazed nearby. Countless seasons of fallen leaves and the excess earth from burials had washed there over decades and layered down into a rich topsoil that would have been priceless in gardens on the valley floor. Now it produced only weeds among its crumbling stones.

The current fence surrounding the cemetery was modern, and paid for mostly by my father and a few of the other descendants who had consciences. To the right of the gate stood the ruins of an unfinished cinder block shelter for the elders of the church, erected to replace an old wooden structure that had become dangerously rotted during the 1960's. Unfortunately, there was no top on the shelter because work on it had ceased when the church members decided they would no longer meet there.

Summer meetings were discontinued when one of the church members, my great-great Aunt Gracie Prater, began to be visited during services by her estranged husband, John P. They had long had a tempestuous relationship, which worsened when their son Ghomer died in World War II. It became worse when another son, Leonard, was shot to death, and Gracie joined the church. John P was incensed. Some of their discussions on the future of their marriage would occur during church services, and would often result in the sound of open hands on faces. This pattern culminated with a particularly tense episode for the faithful when John P arrived with pistol in hand and invited them to leave the cemetery, which they promptly did, never to return.

The outdoor services held on the Old Prater were not unique to the mountain culture, and in fact were common, but would have appeared alien to churchgoers today who demand cushioned pews and carpeted floors. While the preachers held forth from the shelter, the congregation sat on benches between the graves, cooling their faces in the summer heat with cheap paper fans supplied by the local funeral homes. As a child, I would often slip away from my mother or one of my grandmothers who was assigned the unwelcome task of keeping me occupied and play in the small stone-filled world around me. I had just begun to memorize names on the stones when I quit, determining, because of my new knowledge of Grandpaw Harrison's questionable pedigree, that I may not have been as closely related to them as I thought.

And now, whatever I had learned as a child, I had forgotten, or so I thought, and I approached my work on the cemetery as if I were visiting it for the first time.

But there were things I could not forget, and they began to reappear as I walked through the cemetery gate. I also began to notice new things about the layout of the cemetery. The lower part, the flattest part of the cemetery was occupied mostly by Prater graves. Farther back and to the right, where the ground rose and fell sharply, were the Hopkins graves. To the left of them was mostly the tangled growth of years of neglect, although there were a few graves hidden in the wild thatch that covered that section. My father had always required my brother or me to take flowers to those graves, for he did not want to see any grave unremembered.

Even before my father died, I noted there were fewer Praters coming to visit, even though they had more family graves. And now, as I walked through the Prater section, I saw few flowers, unlike the small Hopkins section that was always decorated, farther up the hill. Perhaps the Hopkins were simply more zealous about remembering their dead, I thought. After all, it was not easy to get to this place. And besides, there were other Prater cemeteries on Greasy Creek. My great-grandfather Peter had buried a son on the Old Prater near his ancestors, but later started a new cemetery near his home further on up the creek. I often thought that if Peter gave up his son's grave, there must have been much bitterness among his family over this patch of land.

Regardless of family feuds, there was no one on Greasy Creek who could not share some tenderness about someone buried on the Old Prater. And what made this place so special to me, so special that it came yet to me in dreams? What twist of fate gave me the responsibility to assist in its destruction? It was easy to justify moving the cemetery; the road meant progress, and Greasy Creek had languished in a poor economy for the better part of a century. Some sacrifices are always made for progress, and this cemetery would be one of them. And how much of a sacrifice would it be to move these nearly forgotten earthen tombs to a place where family might return to visit them?

But why was it being moved now, when there was no one else to identify the unknown graves? It was naturally unsettling to consider moving the cemetery. I knew that only a few of the bodies in these graves were buried in steel vaults, which would have made for easy relocation. The rest had been 'put away,' as we called it, in simple caskets, usually wooden and usually homemade. When these souls were laid to rest, it was assumed that there would never be a need for movement, and they would return to the earth, dust to dust as the Scripture said, and dust was probably all that was left under most of these stones.

I was not familiar with the thearchy of souls; was there any reason for a spirit to linger near the grave of its body after its elements had dissolved? And how could a name be assigned to a thin layer of black dirt under a rock marker that gave no clues to a novice researcher like me?

I had assets, however, and I began to list them as soon as I realized the enormity of my job. First, there was Maggie Prater Oliver, who had been researching the clans much longer than I had. Maggie was a Hopkins descendant on her mother's side and the daughter of Charles Ed Prater, the son of Perry Prater, and the great-grandson of Ezekial, for whom the cemetery was named. Perry was also the last husband of my grandmother Rissie. When Rissie and Perry wed, they had both been widowed with grown children and they had no children from their union. Rissie, however, with the maternal instinct that she was famous for on the creek, immediately took Perry's children as her own, and assumed the role she had first played with my father.

She told me once of how she felt about her children. It was another of the many family stories that eased her grandchildren into sleep. Not long after she married Perry, he harshly beat Charles Ed for some minor infraction and she stepped between them. Perry began to raise his hand, possibly to her as well, but she coldly informed him that if he touched Charles Ed again, she would leave him on the spot. Perry was angered, as he was unaccustomed to being rebuked, but seeing the fire in her eyes, he yielded and Rissie became the mother Charles Ed had yearned for since his own hemorrhaged to death from tuberculosis in front of him. Like me, Maggie became Rissie's grandchild, part of the extended family Rissie had nurtured over generations, and her research into the family was my first guidance into who we were and where we came from.

43

Maggie had the answers to many of the questions I had about both the Hopkins and Praters and we still gleefully share with each other when we make a new discovery.

There were others who helped. Gail Mays, nee Coleman, who was known to her students when she taught as "Mother Mays" was another great help. Charlene had been one of her students in high school and remembered her as a stern but iconoclastic teacher, a regional feminist who encouraged her students to achieve regardless of the social conditions that could have easily brought them down. When I started my work, I knew she would be invaluable. She lived next to her daughter in Pikeville in a small mobile home filled with books and boxes of files and pictures, mostly of the Coleman family we were both part of. Her father Milton Coleman was my great-grandfather Paris' brother, and was part of the exodus of Colemans who left Greasy after her mother shot her uncle dead. She traveled all over the United States before coming back to Pike County to teach school and live out her life.

She was the first one to introduce me to David Coleman, our shared ancestor and my great-great-great grandfather, a Union soldier in the Civil War. He was an unusual sort, and moved from Greasy Creek, in the southeast of Pike County, to Peter Creek, in the Northeast, and back every few years.

"I don't know why he did that," she said. I later discovered why, but it was too late to share the news with her.

We had been working together for two years when I picked up the paper and read her obituary. There had been no funeral service and her body had been donated to science. That was Gail in her element, I thought. As much as she helped me with what was becoming a quest to make sure my family's bodies were properly treated, she cared nothing about the disposition of her own.

Another great help was Mary Wright, whose mother, Clarinda, was named for her grandmother Clarinda Adkins Phillips, the wife of Zachariah Phillips, a Confederate soldier. "Zach" and "Clary" were also two of my great-great-great grandparents on my mother's side. At first, I recalled little that I had been told about them, except that Zach had red hair and was killed by Clary's cousin Winright Adkins. My sister named her first son "Zachary," as was the spelling on Clary's tombstone: "Wife of Zachary Phillips" When my sister's second son was born, he had red hair, like his brother's namesake, but since "Zachariah" was already used, she gave him another family name and Daniel Jackson Prater, our great-great grandfather had a namesake as well. "Dan'l Jack" was buried on the Old Prater near his father Ezekiel. "Zeke" was a Union cavalryman, and comrade of David Coleman, and at one time Zach's enemy.

Until the Civil War ended, Zach and Clary lived in a cabin on the valley floor, not far from the little cemetery below the Old Prater. During my research, I came upon an old death record from 1856, in which I learned they had lost two infant children who were probably buried there. I finally had a name to go with the indelible image of the hogs urinating on the cemetery, and I began to feel my grandmother's anger all over again.

I had learned there was more of a paper trail to my family than I thought, but I learned even more from Mary. She helped me see into the long buried past, into another age, into the great conflict of the American Civil War, and I was surprised at what I found. I thought my family had no part in the Civil War, but indeed they had, on both sides of the issue.

Mary was close to that hidden past, and remembered keenly the conversations of her childhood, conversations in which it was revealed, sometimes reluctantly, because it was still a painful topic. It was now painful to me because I had ignored it.

My blanket condemnation of Greasy Creek and my rejection of my ancestry in my youth had cost me many memories, and in one case, a great treasure. Another great-uncle, Jerome Brown, known simply as "Brown" to everyone in the family, was one of the most intelligent men I ever met. He married my grandmother Lexie Prater's sister Enid before the Great Depression and they moved to Florida in 1928, to Orlando, which was known then as The City Beautiful. In the 1930's, when the economy folded in Florida, they came back to Greasy Creek so that Brown could teach in the Pike County schools. He taught my mother in several grades before immigrating back to Florida when the economy picked up. Until his death, he called her "Pancake," the pet name he crafted for her when she was his favorite student.

In 1970, Brown left Enid to come back to Pike County to write his memoirs, and he had plenty to write about. He had served in the Army in World War I, in the Navy in World War II, and in the Coast Artillery between the wars, but he was most interested in the people of Greasy Creek. He took a room in an old two-story house that began life as a log cabin and was rebuilt many times, and sat down with a small typewriter to attempt a sort of Greasy Creek Anthology. He knew the Greeks well, and may have envisioned himself as a more modern Edgar Lee Masters. I often visited, and he would regale me with stories of the creek, especially of the Hamlins and Praters and other families whose blood I shared. It was fun to listen, but I made no notes: Brown had asked me to publish his memoirs should he die before getting them into print and I promised I would, although without much enthusiasm.

He moved back to Florida and was dead by 1985, when I called Enid during a business trip to Orlando. She lived in the same house she and Brown bought when they first moved there, and it was filled with the memorabilia of their lives. After Brown died, Enid married again and that husband was also gone, his ashes sealed in a small urn on the metal marker she had purchased for Brown's grave.

Enid picked me up at my hotel for a white-knuckle excursion through traffic during which she expressed her disdain for the Disney-era interlopers who had sullied her City Beautiful. Enid, exercising the privilege of a grand matron of the old town, seemed to enjoy pulling out into traffic without looking both ways. Actually, I don't recall her looking either way. This exercise resulted in more than a few execrations in Spanish along with uplifted middle fingers. She happily paid them no mind, and we somehow got home. After my heart rate slowed, I inquired about the manuscript.

"Aunt Enid," I asked, "what happened to the book Brown was working on? He put a lot of work into that."

She made a dismissive gesture with her hand.

"Oh, that. I burned it," she said. "Nobody needs to read that old stuff."

Burned it? Damn, I thought, that was supposed to have been mine.

I was a bit miffed that she had not given me the manuscript Brown had promised, or more correctly, that I had promised Brown I would publish, but it was not enough to spoil my visit. I recalled that incident as I passed through the Prater section of the cemetery.

When it occurred, it seemed a minor loss. Now it was catastrophic.

I suspect one of the things she did not want anyone to read was the story of Hester Prater Adkins, the most beautiful of my great-grandfather's sisters, and who had one of the most impressive stones on the Old Prater. A marble spire with an open Bible on its crown, Hester's brothers erected it after her husband murdered her in 1924. It was a great family scandal.

Eli Adkins owned a boarding house in Pikeville and suspected his wife of supplying more than room and board to one of their boarders. Eli left for work one day and after getting off the train, without Hester knowing it, slipped silently into his house to have his suspicions confirmed. He took a long-barreled .45 pistol out of the holster he left hanging on the kitchen door and killed them both with one shot, the bullet entering the back of the boarder's skull, exiting his right eye and entering Hester's left eye before stopping in the back of her skull. He left them as he found them and brought the city police back to present the scene to them.

He then sent word to Hester's brothers, including my great-grandfather Peter Prater, to come for her body.

He was never prosecuted and married again not long afterward.

Even the newspaper story took his side. It could have been the general attitude toward women as chattel, or it could have been that he was wealthy enough to have political connections. In Kentucky then, one could get away with murder if well connected. I often think it could be done today. The political corruption in Kentucky since the Civil War has been legendary.

Hester's brothers raised a monument to her spirit, but none of her children are buried near her. Eli forbade them from mentioning her name while he was alive. Sadly, none of her descendants had decorated her grave in years. I wondered if the only thing remaining of her in that grave was Eli's bullet.

There is an old picture of Hester, taken at least a decade before her death, at the funeral of one of her sisters, three of them now buried on the Old Prater near her. Standing in the picture is her father, Daniel Jack, who holds his now motherless granddaughter, and her mother Melissa, who holds another one. Around them are her brothers, some of whom are now buried near her as well. Hester, with grief etched on her lovely face, is on the porch behind the family gathering, and nearby, with an unmistakable air of boredom, is Eli. It is not hard to see the distance between them.

When Hester was killed, Peter was the caretaker of the cemetery, but afterwards moved up the creek to his own property where he began a new cemetery for his family, even though his first child was buried on the Old Prater. Why did he not bury any more of his own family there? His parents, grandparents, brothers and sisters slept on the Old Prater. Was it because of Hester's murder and the continuing bitterness over her husband's actions? Maybe, or maybe he simply no longer wanted to deal with his brother Jim. Peter did return every year to decorate his son's grave and to whitewash the gravehouse he had erected over his father's grave. I remembered the gravehouse, with its small window where one could look through for reassurance the grave was still there.

I looked at the cemetery differently now, and realized I would never look at it the same again. Every time I had been there previously, it was much like walking into a familiar house, where you would not take notice of the furniture unless there was something new. The Old Prater had been that familiar to me and since 1983, when we buried my grandmother Laura, nothing had changed, but now I knew there would never be another burial here. In fact, soon there would be no graves here at all.

Unlike before, I could no longer take things for granted. This cemetery would soon be gone, I thought, and it was imperative to make sure all the dead were identified. There was no one left who knew every burial, and I knew there were burials here without markers. Over the years, family visits had withered away, and even once a year was more frequent than many people could or would afford. As a result, the graves that were once scraped and mounded every year, to make them appear new and to relive the deceased's story, were soon lost to the grass and vines.

The main cemetery path ran from the gate to the Hopkins plot, crossing in front of Zeke's Union headstone and behind Henry D. Adkins' stone, also government issued. Henry D was Zeke's best friend from the old 39th Kentucky, and had married Elisha Hopkins' daughter Bethina before the War, but afterward they divorced and no one knew where she was buried. Could a final forgiveness on one of their parts have placed them back together after death? That was another question I could not answer without seeing what the earth yielded when the cemetery was moved.

To the left of the Hopkins plot above me was a vast area of weeds and brush that was now rarely cut away. An exception was Harlen Damron's grave at the upper left edge of the cemetery with its tall, white tombstone and its small but amazingly clear photograph of Harlen imbedded in the stone. I knew of no other Damron graves in the cemetery, but Harlen had agreed to be buried there since Rissie wanted to be buried near her mother and father.

She had selected Harlen's gravesite well, I thought as I sat beside his marker and looked down over the cemetery. In the valley below, where the new school now stood and where the old, three-room Middle Greasy School had once stood, nearly everyone buried here had played as children. Perhaps Rissie had been courted by Harlen in that schoolyard; perhaps everyone on the creek had learned what love was all about there.

I took out the plat given me and began checking off the graves. Obviously, not all the graves were recorded. Indeed, it would take someone who knew that a grave was there to find it, and I certainly did not know them all. A cursory examination would reveal little, and I began taking notes to pass on later to the KYDOT. It would cost the US 460 Reconstruction Project a little more than was budgeted for grave removal, I could tell them.

And of all the roads needing improvement in Pike County, why was my favorite road causing me such grief? US 460, like every other road in this tired place, had basically one function: to take young people away when the coal industry waned. Before the mines came, the primitive roads brought people into the hills on horses or oxen. They planned to stay; some did and some went on. When the mines came, they came again. But the boom-and-bust cycles of the mining industry changed attitudes, and people began to wonder why they should linger.

As I was growing up, the main roads were, to be charitable, unimproved. Miserable, pot-holed, narrow strips of gravel and tar with no shoulders, they were only marginally better and sometimes worse than the dirt roads. Every year, hordes of Pike County's new high school graduates fled over them in June, looking for jobs in some other place. In the 1970's the Arabs shut off the oil spigots and coal became important again. New mines opened and new roads were built to haul away the primordial fuel that the mountains yielded. Some of the roads had already been converted to four-lanes. US 460 was the last to be upgraded, and it was the road that took me away, a quarter-century before, for what I thought was the final time.

I had left once before, in 1965 when I used US 23 to go to Akron where we had once lived and where the Robinsons now lived, but I returned four years later, tiring of the Ohio winters and the fast pace of Northern life. In 1970, after my first marriage collapsed, I left for what I swore would be forever, heading east, into Virginia. Of all the places I had ever visited, I loved Virginia the most, and ironically, it was on US 460 in that state that I lived until I returned in 1975.

Originally built from Norfolk, Virginia to St. Louis, Missouri, 460, as both Virginians and Kentuckians refer to the road, passes through Appomattox, where the South began its death rattle with Lee's surrender. The National Park there is still known locally and wistfully as "the surrender grounds." It then passes through Lynchburg, where I lived for five years, absorbing the Civil War history of the region, and never thinking my old home in Pike County had anything to do with that great conflict. I was now learning that it did, and I also learned my ancestors had driven cattle from Pike County all the way to Lynchburg across the same route that became 460, a hundred years before I arrived there. The road itself had changed, of course, but the route was much the same, although truncated to Frankfort, Kentucky with the building of a new Interstate to Missouri. Neglected throughout Kentucky, 460 had already been upgraded in Virginia when the KYDOT finally made its move.

SPIRITS IN THE FIELD

I might not have lived in Lynchburg but for a timely automobile accident. At Christiansburg, Interstate 81 crosses 460 and I turned my MG onto it to take a side trip up to Lexington to visit Bobby James, a Kentucky friend who later became my brother-in-law. After too much beer and pizza, I followed him home, his taillights dim in front of me, and on a blackened curve, I became airborne and crossed over what appeared to be a pickup truck under my headlights.

I came down in a cow pasture near two Rockbridge Countians who had been sitting in the truck, genially passing a bottle between them.

"You OK, son?" they inquired, after rushing over to my window.

"I think so," I replied.

"Well, you'd better have a drink before you see the front of yo' cah."

I was unhurt, and although the damage was ugly, my car was not ruined. After we pushed the bumper away from the tires, I found I could move and went on to Bobby's house.

"Where you been?" he asked when I came in.

"Having a drink with the locals," I said before crashing into his couch.

The next morning I awoke with the hope that it was all a bad dream, but an inspection of my car disabused me of that hope. I had heard an advertisement for a MG dealer in Lynchburg, back on 460, and I said good-bye to Bobby and drove across the Blue Ridge to have my car checked out. The damage was cosmetic and the car was sound, but it would take a few days to repair so I had to stay over. Suddenly realizing my mortality and my need for a job, I remembered a school board sign I had seen in neighboring Amherst County.

In Pike County, I had been a teacher, using my father's political contacts for a job just as everyone else did. I did not expect to be hired in this new place since I had no family there and no political clout, but I thought I would give it a try.

I was hired the day I walked in.

That fact merely added to the disillusionment I had with Kentucky's infamous corruption and I swore again never to return. A year later, I married Bobby's sister Roberta and we returned to Virginia's 460 to live. In spite of my oaths, we came back in 1975. A year later, we divorced and Roberta returned to Virginia alone.

This project is dredging up too many memories, I thought.

Why did 460 have to come through Greasy Creek? Why did it have to be the same road I traveled on endlessly, courting Roberta, telling her how beautiful Virginia was and how we would never want to live anywhere else, only to see her drive away on that road when we parted?

I still can't figure that out, I thought.

If I can't do that, with that memory still smoldering, how can I determine who was buried here a hundred years before I was born?

The new 460 would be alien to this old place, far more technologically advanced than the road I left on so many times and light-years ahead in transportation from the road my ancestors knew. After all, they rode horses then.

Like most Southern boys, I grew up around horses. My Uncle Avery Prater, my mother's oldest brother, lived in the hollow above our home and kept magnificent horses that would prance and snort impatiently when he stopped to take my brother or me for a ride.

It was a great thrill to have him stop in front of our house and wait for my brother or me to come out, and an even greater thrill to have him reach down with his great hands to swoop me up into the saddle. There was usually a trace of alcohol on his breath at those times, which merely added to the excitement, in spite of my mother's hand-wringing while we were gone. But he would always bring us back safely and tenderly deposit us on the road before he would touch his horse's flanks with his spurs, causing it to rear up before charging off in a dust cloud.

Avery was my father's best friend, and resembled my mother more than any of his other sisters. Perhaps they simply shared more DNA than the others, but there was always a special bond between the siblings. It was good, I thought, that my father and his brother-in-law were close.

Avery died of Lou Gehrig's Disease before my father succumbed to diabetes, and his decline was perhaps more painful, since his disease was unintelligible to us. At least we could see my father's infirmity, while my uncle was wasting from some faceless killer that left his great frame intact but useless.

Once, while I was helping him pee into his bedpan, he waved his ruined arms toward a pencil and paper he kept near his bed.

"You want to write something, Unk?" I asked as I retrieved them.

With the last strength he had in his hands, he scribbled these words: "Get gun. Shoot me."

I blanched and stared at the note before I crumpled it and put it in my pocket.

"I'm sorry, Bubber," I said, reverting to the special name we had for him as children. "I can't."

I wonder if he ever forgave me.

Avery was a combat engineer in World War II, serving in the same theater as my father, and even saw him on the odd occasion. As the German Army dissolved in front of the relentless American advance, their fuel supplies exhausted, they turned to horses for transportation. As the war ended, Avery's heart fell more from watching those animals die from starvation than watching the scarecrow German soldiers surrender to him. Although he, like my father, loved cars and possessed a grand Hudson Hornet with massive chrome air horns on each front fender, he loved horses more. In his last year, he would watch longingly as the few horses left on Greasy Creek were ridden up his hollow and he would pine for the days when he could sit upright and ride his great animals for everyone to see.

I loved horses too, but could never bring myself to wear spurs when I rode or to whip a horse to make it go faster. With the coming of asphalt on the dirt roads of Greasy Creek, horses were imperiled by the hard surfaces when they tried to stop; I saw too many horses terrified when they slipped that way. And I do not recall one instance of seeing my father or my grandfather on a horse. Even when plowing was done, my father would hire someone else to do it and they would turn their heads when the plowman lashed his beast. With these reasons, and because my family could never afford horses, I did not yearn for one as much as a Georgia or a Tennessee boy might have and I would never allow myself to fall in love with horses.

Except for one.

I met her when my grandfather took me to the old Pikeville Stock Market to look at cattle. Though a strip shopping mall sits there now, until the 1950's the Stock Market was a giant, rickety wooden building with a massive tin roof suspended on whole logs set upright in the ground. Every Thursday, mountain farmers would bring their horses and cattle in from the hollows for a sale that lasted all day. Inside, the men argued over their animals, while the women outside, where truck beds and car trunks offered household necessities, haggled over the prices of domestic items.

I had grown bored and was leaning over the rail at the back of the arena when my eyes were drawn to some activity near a back corridor of the huge structure. There was a great brown and white mare standing obediently by her owner who was negotiating with a prospective buyer. She was fully saddled with dark leather and silver trim and she stood hands high above either man. Across the distance of half a football field, her eyes locked onto me and seemed to know me as a kindred spirit. Before I knew it, I was making my way through the labyrinth of stalls to reach her as she stood, following my every move.

She was even taller than I thought; I could not have raised a foot to the stirrups by myself. As I drew closer, her ears stood up anticipatingly, as if I were an old friend approaching with an apple hidden somewhere in my pocket. Eventually, I was beside her, almost ready to raise my hand to her flared nose, when her owner turned suddenly to me.

"Boy, come here," he said.

Uh-oh. I'm in trouble, now.

"Here, get on this mare and take her up to the gate and back."

I could only stare incredulously. He looked at me quizzically and spoke again.

"Come on, son. You can ride, can't you?"

I managed to nod and without a further word he lifted me into the saddle for what was the most exultant experience of my life.

I took the reins and wheeled the horse around, giving it is head for the short distance to the gate. It snorted, reared slightly, and we sailed away as if we were a pas-de-deux in a great ballet. At the end of my ride I stopped, wheeled around, and returned to the men watching me. I could not believe my good fortune. *Had this really happened?*

The owner lifted me off the mare and I was dismissed with perfunctory thanks. I did not even know her name, but I felt something of mine, something rare and incalculably precious, had been lost to me forever. Even at my age, I knew I could not run to my grandfather and make him buy that magnificent animal. I could only stand and watch as money was exchanged and the horse was led away by its new master. She looked back at me as they rounded a corner, as if asking why I was abandoning her. My eyes swam and it was all I could do to keep from crying. I did later, and had I not been in the company of men, I would have then. It was much like what was being done to me now on the cemetery, and I felt just as helpless.

As helpless as these poor souls are, I thought.

Like Harlen, everyone buried here had been young once, and had their loves and losses. Because of his youth, he reminded me of a line from Housman: *And round that early-laureled head, shall flock to gaze the strengthless dead.* Harlan had died young, and when Rissie buried him, she expected to join him for eternity. But the dead have no strength, no way to combat the forces that can abbreviate eternity to a few generations, and now I could do little for them.

My perch at Harlen's grave had always been my favorite spot on the cemetery. As I looked down at the Hopkins plot from it, I began to wonder why Harrison was not buried next to his mother. Rissie told me that Mammy (her name for her grandmother Dorcus) and Joseph, Harrison's younger brother, were buried somewhere else. There had to be someone important to Harrison in this cemetery for him to select this place for his final resting place, but who was it?

Just another question I had no answer for.

Could I ever do justice to all these mysteries? The earthly remains of real people, my people, would be pulled from a slumber perhaps a hundred years old, and there was nothing I could do about it. The dead were strengthless and I was a poor champion for them. I could have done so much more if I had not once had the bane of youth to lure me away from responsibility. I was now in middle age and felt as worthless as I did when they led away my horse decades before.

But I was determined to do my job, even if it had not been of my choosing. I wrenched open the cells of my memories and began to sift through what fell out. One of the things I remembered was a plot inside the Old Prater, almost in its center, that had long ago disappeared. Behind the row of Hopkins graves where my grandfather lay was once an old wood-and-wire fence that supposedly had graves, although there was nothing inside it. I once asked my father who was buried there, and he said he did not know, but it was Hopkinses. Mamaw Rissie said it was the Old Ones, whatever that meant. The old fence was now gone, the grave houses were gone, and the cemetery seemed more still than I ever remembered it. There was family here that I had never known, and not just the graves that were marked.

There were other spirits here, in this lonely field on this high mountainside and they called me as surely as a dinner bell once called men from the cornfields that had disappeared from Greasy Creek.

I knew what I had to do: I would create a "possible" list of everyone who might be buried next to a burial here. A wife, of course, and children, perhaps a mother or father. If I could determine they were buried somewhere else, then they would be removed from the possible list. *My god, I thought, this could take forever.* Census records, old marriage licenses, wills, deeds; I had no idea how much research would be required. And I knew only that I did not have forever. The backhoes could be unloaded tomorrow for all I knew. I had to hurry.

But another thought entered my mind: am I even worthy of doing this work? I could note how the cemetery had changed over the years, but how had I changed? When Jessie died, my first wife Linda came with me to bury him. When Frank died, Roberta was by my side. And when his second wife, my grandmother Laura died, it was Charlene who walked with me to the grave. Did these spirits, if they were there, have any reason to trust me at all? Had I demonstrated I was too fickle to be entrusted with secrets from beyond the pale? At least I didn't have as many women as Elisha.

Elisha again. Why did I just think of him? I had not heard his name used familiarly since Rissie died.

Perhaps it is fitting that this cemetery is moved for a road, I rationalized, and will be moved to a better place. I would have never allowed the mine operating nearby to touch these graves.

Avery once told a coal company that he would kill anyone who even prospected his land, although, like most Eastern Kentuckians, he did not own the coal under it. But this was different, it was for a greater good, and it would have its benefits. *But there is no one left to tell me who is buried here. There are no spirits rising from their graves to tell me their stories. Greasy Creek flows into the Big Sandy, not the Spoon.*

As I rose from my seat beside Harlen's grave, the hairs rose on my neck. I had the odd sensation I was not alone, but I looked around and could see nothing.

It might have been the wind or merely an odd thought resonating from some incompletely discharged synapse, but I thought I heard someone distinctly say: *Elisha.*

Whoa, I thought.

Elisha? Elisha Hopkins? Ol' Lige, Greasy Creek's most famous reprobate?

I heard it again, from a different part of the cemetery.

Elisha.

Then another voice, with an additional argument: *Elisha is the key.*

How could Elisha be the key? The key to what? He isn't even buried here.

Elisha.

"What the hell is going on?" I said out loud to no one in particular, and the whispering stopped. I now heard only the wind rustling the autumn leaves.

"Did someone just speak to me?" I asked. "Or I am going crazy?"

But there were no more voices.

I silently apologized to the spirits that may have heard my intemperate comment.

I checked for ticks when I got back to my Jeep and made a mental note to research Lyme Disease to see if hallucinations were one of its symptoms. I rarely heard my father curse, and I wondered where I got my predilection for casual swearing. I turned the vehicle around and started to head back off the hill when I stopped and rolled down the window for one last look through the cemetery gate.

Who is buried here, I wondered? Are they all my family? The only one I knew who wasn't related was a Civil War soldier named Bracken, who came here as an old man in 1920 with his daughter and son-in-law who worked in the Greasy Creek mine. If one stranger were here, there may be others. There could be immigrant graves, graves of men who came from strange places to work inside these hills and who died here without family to mourn their passing.

There are soldiers here, men who went away from Greasy Creek to war, to fight for a country that was barely formed when the cemetery was new. This is the one place that confirmed to me that I am not an orphan since my father died— the one place where all that was good and real on Greasy Creek was safe from the awful world surrounding it. It overlooks the field where white men and women came and went for two hundred years. And for how many thousand years, I asked, the Indians before them? This is not just a cemetery; it is a crossroads, an American crossroads. Greasy Creek saw generations come and go, sometimes stopping and sometimes not, and even today, its children have little reason to stay.

But the cemetery, eternal and unchanging as the world around it metamorphosed again and again, was a reason to return. And now it too would soon be swept up in change.

And I do not know even how many graves it holds, nor who is buried in half of them.

Could Elisha help me understand these mysteries, I thought? Of course he could, but he's been dead for nearly a century.

Perhaps he was the key; perhaps he had something to do with this cemetery, regardless of the fact he is not buried here. And if anyone would tell me the truth it would be Elisha.

Where are you, old man, when I need you?

If there were anyone unconcerned with polite society, anyone who would not have covered up the truth or burned a manuscript because no one needed to read that old stuff, it would have been you. Why don't you give me a hand?

Expecting no response from my taunt, and hearing none, I put the Jeep in gear and headed off to the mountain.

Hooker

For two years after I received the first plat of the cemetery, I plagued all my living elders for information about the family until I exhausted all their resources and most of their patience. I haunted the courthouse archives in Pikeville and the state archives in Frankfort looking for whatever scrap of information I could find about the Hopkins of Greasy Creek. I had become well known to the ladies who worked at the courthouse, and after a while they stopped charging me for copies of old marriage certificates. "Just give us a copy of your research," they would say.

I became very familiar to several college librarians who were accustomed to my arriving shortly before closing and scribbling notes furiously. When I had more time, I spun the reels on their microfilm readers until my eyes glazed over. I learned to decipher the century-old handwriting of census enumerators with great skill.

I poured over message boards on the Internet and sent out inquiries to distant places asking for word on this person or that person, all the time attempting to gain some information for the theories I had postulated on the unknown graves. I visited graveyards and took reams of notes on the tombstones I read there, and then turned again repeatedly to my relatives, hounding family members in four states for whatever information I could glean. There were no clues I would not seize upon and follow with a desperate resolve.

But my leads were playing out, and I was beginning to feel I had accomplished little. Time became my enemy.

I had identified several graves, but there was still the mystery of the lost plot in the center of the cemetery, and I had no facts. I confirmed the plot existed; everyone agreed it was there and the Hopkins family would tend in the old days, but I still had only conjecture to assist me, no facts, no stones, nothing concrete.

By now I had formed a theory, and the closer I looked at it, the more it seemed plausible: the plot must be the final resting-place of Cornelius and Dorcus Hopkins, the first Hopkins settlers in Pike County. They had lived on their land grant on the river at the mouth of Greasy Creek for forty years, but sometime during the Civil War, Elisha brought them deeper into Greasy Creek for their own safety. After the War, they still lived there, somewhere near the Old Prater Cemetery, and I suspect that was where their graves were. But only a forensic anthropologist would have been able to confirm that to me, and I had no assurance the KYDOT would give me that help.

Hooker Prater, Jim Prater's son, lived next to the lower cemetery, and had grown up with me playing among the stones on the Old Prater. He was the last Prater to keep up the Prater graves, in spite of the fact his father clearly indicated he did not appreciate his work. Hook, as everyone called him, remembered the mystery plot as well, and believed it to be big enough to hold at least a dozen graves, but he had no other information. No one did, and I grieved for my youth when Rissie could have told me everything I now wanted so desperately to know.

The exact boundary of the plot was lost to time since the fence had fallen years ago. I have an old picture of my father as a small child standing next to his mother's tombstone, and behind him the old fence is clearly visible. Hook told me it had been taken down in the 1950's.

So the existence of the center plot in the cemetery was documented; but that was all. Extrapolating a little, I concluded it must have been someone close to Harrison. It was clear to me that there had to be some reason for him to bring his clan to the

Old Prater for burial, and it had to be because there were Hopkins there first; most likely, Cornelius and Dorcus. The plot had little to distinguish it now. There was no mounding to speak of since the accumulation of a hundred years of leaf fall had filled in any depressions, and no one remembered stones in there when the fence was still up. Perhaps the other graves, if they existed, were of Cornelius and Dorcus' children who had died between the censuses I had nearly committed to memory.

Something noteworthy was the fact that Cornelius and Dorcus moved *during* the Civil War. From the census records I determined their last home was roughly the location of the Old Prater Cemetery. I suspect the violence of that war and the constant threat of foraging made it untenable for them to live near the river, which was the major transportation route in the Nineteenth Century. My research kept leading back to the Civil War, the seminal event in American history, and I was learning daily how devastating it had been to the mountain region, and to the families of Greasy Creek. In my arrogance, I blithely assumed Eastern Kentucky had no Civil War experience. *Not in this backward place, I thought. No JEB Stuarts would have emerged from here.*

But I was rapidly learning more about Greasy Creek than I ever knew existed. And with each discovery, I would hear faint echoes of stories Rissie had told me years before.

Were Cornelius and Dorcus the Old Ones she spoke of, I wondered? Were they those incomplete figures I saw waiting for me near Harrison's grave in my dream?

Maggie Oliver had introduced me to Joseph Hopkins, brother to Columbus Christopher Hopkins and Elisha Hopkins, great-great-great grandfathers, respectively, of her and me. We knew that Joseph had been killed in Confederate service, and through my census research, I learned that Lucinda, his widow, eventually returned to Greasy Creek from Shelby Creek where their family had lived since the 1850's. But I knew little more about them. I could not find her grave, and postulated that it might have been near Cornelius and Dorcus. Two of her great-grandchildren were buried just below the mystery plot, while the rest of that family was buried on up the creek. There was something about Joseph and Lucinda that intrigued me.

I called Randall Osborne, a retired Pike County schoolteacher and one of the best local historians, for more information.

"Randall, what can you tell me about Joseph Hopkins, Corporal 10th Kentucky CSA?" I said into the telephone receiver.

"Joseph Hopkins," he said. "Now where have I heard that name before?"

"He was captured and shot by the enemy October 1, 1864, according to the information I have," I replied. "Must have been at Saltville."

Randall knew well the regiments that fought at Saltville, one of the fiercest battles fought between Eastern Kentuckians, even though it was fought in Virginia, over the only source of salt remaining for the Confederacy in the last years of the war. Randall had written histories for some of the regiments that fought there.

"Joseph Hopkins," he said again. "Nah, there's something else."

"He's supposed to be buried in the Veteran's Cemetery at Louisa," I said.

"Which doesn't exist," he added.

"Bingo, some more errata from the old Registration Project," I said.

The Graves Registration Project was a New Deal endeavor that attempted to list the final resting-place of every American in every war. It was, of course, an impossible task, but no one expected it to be successful. The very attempt was, in its own way, a memorial, an overdue act of recognition for the patriots who bled and died for their country, even before it became a country. It was also a way for President Roosevelt to stir up some patriotic fervor, to prepare the country for the war he saw coming. But it was unnecessary to stimulate patriotism after Pearl Harbor, so the project was abandoned in 1942. Even with its errors, the project's data is yet a godsend for researchers.

"Who is Joseph Hopkins?" Randall asked.

"My great-great-great grandfather Elisha Hopkins' brother," I said. "He had three: Joseph, Columbus, who served in the 39th, and John, who didn't serve either side. Neither did Elisha. Hell, he had three families in 1860. I don't guess he could go.

"I think some of Joseph's family is buried on my two cemeteries to be moved, and I don't know where his wife is buried. Somewhere on Greasy, I suspect. She was a Morgan: Lucinda Morgan."

"Joseph Hopkins," he repeated. I could almost hear the bells ringing for Randall. "Wait a minute, let me look something up."

Randall retreated to his archives and was gone no more than a few minutes when he came back to the phone.

"Still there?" he asked with a chuckle to his voice. I knew he had found something.

"Yeah, what'd you find?"

"Your great-great-whatever uncle was one of three men who reported producing over a hundred bales of cotton in the 1860 Pike County agricultural census."

Cotton?

"Say what?" I was incredulous: Pike County was a huge place, but mountainous, its arable land in narrow shelves on its riverbanks. With barely enough land for houses today, there is little room to raise a garden, and even a hundred years ago, with one-tenth the current population, Pike County seemed an unlikely location for such an industry.

"Cotton, damn it. Didn't you know we grew cotton here?"

"In Pike County? No, I didn't."

"Well, neither did I until I saw this census. When I researched this, it all made sense. Apparently the Federal government saw the war coming and in the 1850's started encouraging cotton production above the Mason-Dixon Line," he said. "Wanted to save their asses when the Rebs cut off their cotton supply."

I enjoyed Randall's laconic wit and his obvious Confederate sympathy.

"Indiana and Maryland were about as far north as they could to it successfully," he continued. "I didn't know any of this myself until I got my microfilms and found it. It was pretty interesting when I started reading up on it.

"I found a letter from one of the old boys in an Ohio regiment that came through here in '62 with Garfield. He wrote home about seeing cotton growing, something he had never seen before. Even sent cotton seeds home.

"Looks like your Joseph Hopkins was pretty successful if he could squeeze out a hundred bales of cotton. Where did he live?"

"Somewhere in Shelby Valley," I said. "According to the census records"

"That figures," he replied. "That was the strongest Confederate area. Hang on a minute."

I could hear him flipping open boxes of microfilm and loading another reel into his viewer.

"Got it," he said. "Just what I figured. He lived near Thomas May, big Confederate sympathizer. Hmm. He had a bunch of kids."

"Eight of them," I said. "Seven girls and one boy."

"And he died," Randall said. "Damn shame. Well, that's the way the War went around here. You'll find a lot more of it as you get into this."

The enormity of what happened here still gave Randall pause. He turned to a more contemporary subject.

"How's everything down at the snake pit?" he asked, referring obviously to my place of employment.

"Still full of vipers," I said. "Did you expect anything different?"

"Of course not," he said. Before he hung up, he offered me the usual admonition for workers at the Central Office of the Pike County School System: "Watch your back."

And I was back to square one. I needed help from the KYDOT, and I wasn't getting it. If I could determine from the remains on the Old Prater that the deceased was a man or a woman or a child, it would help me immensely. If I could determine the age of the deceased, it would help me even more. But the KYDOT kept putting me off. No one came right and said, "We can't do it," but I never got a straight answer. *Typical bureaucratic bullshit, I thought.* Hiring someone trained in analyzing remains would cost the state money. It was clear to me they were interested only in moving the known graves, and if there were any unknowns or lost graves, that would be just hard cheese. They weren't going to look for them.

My patience with the KYDOT was beginning to fray, and I suspect they were annoyed at my persistent requests. *What was their problem, I wondered?* The law clearly stated that they had to give me assistance in identifying unknown graves, but I kept getting excuses and evasions. I dutifully passed on the information I collected to them, but I still had no commitment from them to help me identify whatever came out of those graves.

Cemetery removal projects were not uncommon in Pike County. In fact, the Annie E. Young Cemetery, where my father was buried, was established to serve as the relocation cemetery for graves displaced when the U.S. Army Corps of Engineers built the Fishtrap Dam just upriver from Greasy Creek. Hundreds of graves from old mountain cemeteries along the Levisa Fork of the Big Sandy River were moved there, and most of them were identified merely as "Unknown." Those sacred places in dozens of hollows are now flooded and no more research can be done as to who once lay there. I did not want that to happen to my graves, to the dust of my family, if I could prevent it.

I was getting discouraged, and I was, admittedly, nearing the end of my rope. The great resources I could have had were themselves buried beneath the soil of Greasy Creek, and there was no one still alive who could have given me merely the direction I needed to go to gather my information. After the exhilaration of my early success in identifying some of the unknown graves, I was growing depressed from the failures that were now all too common and for the constant reiteration

I would walk the trail up to the cemetery again and again, but there were no more whispered clues from phantom pickets at the gate. When I entered, I would walk to Harlen's grave on the top edge of the cemetery and sit at his feet, looking at the sharp, clear picture of the grandfather I never knew and then face east, as all the graves faced, awaiting the Resurrection. I would study the blank surfaces of the back of my ancestors' tombstones but they revealed no more than the unsounding bones resting under me, and I began to sense failure. From Harlen's grave, the schoolhouse field could be seen clearly, where most of it was obscured from the lower part of the cemetery. The trees had grown over the forty years since my school days, but they could not hide the fact that I had a huge responsibility. There were adults and children buried on the Old Prater and practically all of them once played on that field. Now they rested on this hillside and they could not have comprehended that the eternity they anticipated here would not be eternal at all.

It was not just the obvious unknown graves I could not identify; there were undoubtedly many others, perhaps all of my blood, in this forgotten place, and I could do nothing more to determine their names. My newfound information on the Civil War was interesting, but I yet did not suppose there was any real relevance to me for my cemetery work. I still did not know who was buried in the unknown graves on the Old Prater, and knew even less about the ravaged lower cemetery.

I had become almost resigned to losing those stories forever when my reluctant voyage veered back onto track.

On a fall Saturday evening, my cousin Esther Prater stayed over with Charlene and me, and as we rambled about family, the subject of the Old Prater came up again. Esther, as well as her twin sister Easter, and I grew up together; we were 'blood,' and we both descended from the Union soldier the Old Prater was named for. Easter and Esther were identical twins, ebullient daughters of the redoubtable Jim Prater but with none

69

of their father's misanthropism. They remembered nothing of the Hog Pen Incident. The Twins, as everyone knew the insep- arable pair on Greasy Creek, and I had graduated from high school together and we even resembled each other in our youth; black hair, tall with dark complexions, like most Praters.

Over the past few years Esther and I had grown close. Since neither the twins nor I had children, we probably felt closer to the family we had left, so we often talked of the Praters and shared stories of the Prater eccentricities. The amorousness and legendary parsimony of the clan was always good for a few laughs.

Eventually, the conversation turned to Elisha Hopkins, who we agreed must have been even more amorous than any Prater who ever lived. After all, no one else on Greasy had three families at the same time. That evening she startled me with this question:

"Bruce, did you ever find out what Hooker Hopkins did with his journals?"

"Hooker Hopkins?" I questioned. "Journals? What journals?"

"The ones he wrote on the cemetery," she replied.

"You mean Hooker wrote journals about the cemetery?"

"Yes, but he wrote them *on* the cemetery. He used to go up to the cemetery and stay there all night writing in his journals."

"What?"

Her words were electric. I knew nothing of Hooker's journals, and I knew little of Hooker except for a faded memory of him at his older Brother Will's funeral in 1959. *Hooker wrote journals about the cemetery? He wrote them on the cemetery?* After losing Brown's work, I had despaired of ever having a first-hand account to help me. Hooker Hopkins was one of the last three children of Elisha Hopkins. Where I was only a great-great-great grandchild of Elisha's first marriage in 1833, Hooker was the son of his last marriage in 1879. *Elisha would have told his son about his family, I thought.*

"I never knew about any journals," I said. "In fact, I never knew much about Hooker. Tell me more."

"Well, Hooker used to scare me to death when I was little," she said in her distinctive Southern staccato. "Because he always wore a big, black raincoat and he carried a leather valise with all these little books in it. Once a year he would come back to Greasy, and you could see him going up and down the road visiting people, and at night he would go up to the cemetery and stay up there all night with a lantern and just write."

My heart began to pound; I was sure Esther and Charlene could hear it.

"What did he write about?" I asked.

"I don't know for sure," Esther said. "But Mommy always said he was writing about the people in the cemetery. Sometimes I would go out on the porch late at night and I could see his light up on the cemetery. I thought he was a ghost or something."

I was thrilled, and a little abashed. Here I was, struggling to find out something, anything about the unknown graves in the cemetery, mostly Hopkins graves and I knew nothing about Hooker's journals. They would be the most valuable documents I could hope for, and it took a Prater cousin to tell me about them.

"Did your Mom ever read any of his journals?" I asked.

"No, he kept them to himself. Bruce, do you think they're still around?"

God, I hope so, I thought. This could be the break I need. If this is true, he would have mapped the cemetery, located graves now lost in the overgrowth, probably written something about every one of them. This could prove my theories. More importantly, it could prevent the losses I was grudgingly beginning to accept.

"I don't know," I said, but I knew then that if I had to, I would knock at the gates of Hell itself to see them.

I tried to collect my thoughts about Hooker. I knew little about him other than he lived in a neighboring county, and had a son named Ersel. Beyond that, and the occasional mention of his name at a family reunion, I knew practically nothing. I also remembered wondering, as a child, why we called him Hooker, not Uncle Hooker, as we called his brother Uncle Will.

Uncle Will Hopkins was a different story. Some people on Greasy called him Big Will, some called him Cripple Will because he walked with a cane. I called him Uncle Will because my father did, and he was the first person I ever loved who died. I was twelve years old, and it broke my heart.

Uncle Will lived with Rissie and Perry, her second husband, in his final years, and when he died she made the men on Greasy Creek take him up to Ripley Knob to be buried beside his father. That was what he wanted, but it was not an easy chore. Today, it would take an accomplished hiker an hour to climb Ripley Knob, and in spite of a hundred years of hollowing it out for its coal, I am confident the mountain has not shrunk since 1959.

Before Uncle Will died, my father would occasionally collect the family and Uncle Will for a weekend trip across the state line to Virginia, where Will's daughter Glennel had a restaurant. Mink, as everyone knew her, was a gregarious woman who loved to laugh. On the rare trips she made to Greasy Creek, she would walk into our home and begin washing dishes or clearing off the table as if she were simply a family member assigned a chore. In half the memories I had of her, she would be standing at the kitchen sink, her hands in dishwater, good-naturedly scolding me for being such a hapless lout. She moved to Indiana after giving up on the possibility of making a living in the hills and lived near her brother Victor. She rarely came back to Greasy Creek, and after Uncle Will died, I never saw her again.

His was another funeral at Rissie's house, and after the usual fire-and-brimstone Regular Baptist preaching, we began the journey up the hill to the top of Ripley Knob. Hooker Prater hitched up a team of mules to a sled and carried the casket as far up the mountain as he could. It was a rude hearse, but not unusual for a funeral in the hills

Esther told me how her brother Hooker acquired his nickname. Hooker's real name was James Lloyd Prater, but because he was frightened of Hooker Hopkins as a child, his teasing uncles naturally gave him the nickname "Hooker" and it stuck. While Hooker Prater drove the team, his namesake Hooker Hopkins walked behind the sled carrying his brother to his final rest. The men of the creek carried him the rest of the way to the Knob. All I could do at my age was to carry water for the men who were carrying him, and they rested several times along the way. The image of Uncle Will's coffin on the ground during their breaks is still locked in my mind after all these years.

"I never really knew Hooker," I said. "All I know is that he lived in Floyd County. He was Uncle Will's brother and he had another brother named Paris. They were Elisha's children by his last wife. That's about all I know."

I knew nothing of Paris either, except his name, and that he was buried in a military cemetery somewhere in Tennessee.

"Hooker was very courteous," Esther said. "He would always say, 'Yes, Ma'am when he talked to Mommy."

"Was he a big man, like Uncle Will?" I asked. "I just don't remember."

She thought for a minute, sifting through the collected images of her memory, and then spoke:

"No," she said. "He was kinda short, like the Hopkins were." Again, I wondered where I got my height. And I wondered about Elisha. There is no one left on earth who had actually seen him, except for my great-aunt Bessie in Ohio, who was still in swaddling then. I wondered if the way Elisha treated Harrison was because his grandson was short, and not just because he had a cleft palate. Uncle Will was tall and had big arms and hands and he would smile and hug me when I came into my grandfather Andrew Prater's store before school began in the mornings. I always looked for him behind the coal stove with other old men from the creek. If he were not there in the morning, he would be there in the evening with a nickel or a dime in his trembling fingers for me to purchase a Brown Cow or some other treat.

Esther and I talked late into the night about the old people of Greasy Creek, and then weariness overtook us and she went to bed. Charlene retired soon after, but I stayed up long after they had gone to sleep, and I thought about Elisha and his children. Why did he give Hooker that name? During the Civil War there was Joe Hooker, a Union general, but I had learned none of my family had served in his command. Indeed, fully half of my Civil War ancestors were Confederate, as were most of the soldiers from Greasy Creek. And after I learned what happened to Joseph, I knew there could be no way Elisha would have honored a Union general.

I recalled another conversation with Randall Osborne, who had become a tutor to me on the Civil War in Pike County. This time I surprised him.

"Randall, do you know what I just found out?" I nearly yelled into the telephone receiver in what seemed like the hundredth conversation I had with him after learning about Joseph's cotton farm. "You remember we thought Burbridge's closest victim was that old boy in Johnson County?"

"Yeah?"

"Well, guess what? The reason Joseph isn't buried in Louisa is that he was executed and buried in Bloomfield, way the hell on the other side of Lexington. He died November 7, 1864."

"You're kidding," he said. Randall was suddenly in awe. He knew the stories of General Stephen Burbridge, the Kentucky-born military governor of Kentucky, who faced, along with the Union in Missouri, the most vicious fighting of the Civil War: the internecine and bloody guerrilla warfare that plagued both states.

To quell the guerrilla activity in the Kentucky, Burbridge issued an infamous order that he would shoot four Confederates for every Union soldier "bushwhacked" by rebels. It led to the deaths of over fifty regular Confederates, pulled from their prisons and shot for crimes they usually had nothing to do with. But it did not achieve its desired effect and ultimately President Lincoln dismissed Burbridge from his post because of it. If anything, it hardened the resolve of the

Confederates, and made 1864 the worst year of the War for Kentucky. And it forced Burbridge to flee his native state for Brooklyn, where he died years later, still hated by the state he thought he was saving. In Civil War circles in Kentucky, the debate over Stephen Burbridge still rages.

1864 was a bitter year, and the wounds created then did not heal with Appomattox, but until I made my discovery, no one in Pike County thought that a local boy was one of the fifty-odd victims of Burbridge's tragic mistake.

"Remarkable," Randall said.

"I've even got his execution orders," I told him.

"Remarkable," he repeated. My discovery had rewritten part of Pike County's Civil War history. More importantly, it had reprogrammed my mind away from the indifference I had, for most of my life, displayed toward my family history. Even Randall was impressed.

There was something else. I had concluded from my research that Elisha was very close to his brother Joseph, closer than he was to his brothers Columbus and John, perhaps because Elisha and Joseph were born in Virginia before Cornelius came to Kentucky, and they were business partners as well as brothers. Elisha and Joseph had secured land grants for most of Hopkins Creek, which was named for them.

There was simply no way Elisha Hopkins would have named his son for a Union general.

But Elisha did not name any of his children Joseph, I noted. His daughter Dorcus, my great-great grandmother, named her second son Joseph, after her Uncle Joe, but that Joseph drowned not long after he married in 1893. I was told he drowned in the river while grinding only his second crop of corn.

The only other "Joes" in the family were my great-uncle Bud's son who was killed when he wrecked his pickup truck in 1956, and his son, Joe Jr. Although Joseph was a common name, the Hopkins family did not seem to use it much, as if the name would conjure up memories of things best forgotten.

There was another possibility: I remembered a line from an old Civil War song titled "Jine the Cavalry" that went something like, *Ol' Joe Hooker, come out of the Wilderness, out of the Wilderness, out of the Wilderness.* Could Elisha have heard his brother singing that old Confederate cavalry song, and named his son as a childish prank, much as Hooker Prater had been given his nickname? I was learning not to put anything past Elisha.

But regardless of how Hooker got his name, I promised myself I would get his journals.

Later that night, while lying wide-eyed and looking at the moon through my bedroom skylight, I recalled nights I had stayed with my Prater grandparents and had seen lights on the old cemetery long after dark.

Like my Hopkins grandparents, my Prater grandparents were Old Regulars, but there was a difference in the houses. Rissie's house was always a buzz of activity with people coming in and out constantly. There was always kept food on the dining room table under a big sheet, and almost everyone on the creek stopped in after church to eat. She and Perry smoked constantly and the house kept a sweet tobacco-barn aroma that extended to the upstairs rooms where I would sleep after I got older and was no longer afraid of the dark. There was always the bustle of family and friends slamming the screen door, and always, always laughter.

My grandmother Lexie did not smoke, and would not countenance smokers inside the house and there were, not unexpectedly, fewer visitors. But she read constantly, and there were always *Reader's Digest Condensed Books* around for my hungry mind to absorb. Although there was less conviviality there, her quiet house had its own appeal: fewer visitors meant more time to read without interruption, and I raced through her books until bedtime, their stories permeating my dreams. Some lost memory of a forgotten ghost story from my grandmother's books was probably triggered when I saw the lights on the cemetery

A will o' the wisp, I thought. I had read about them. Or a ghost.

I was afraid to ask my grandparents what it was, for fear of conjuring those demons from the cemetery to perch at the head of my bed.

After all those years, I finally knew what those chimeras, those unacknowledged phantoms of my childhood really were.

When at last I joined Charlene in sleep, I dreamed of honeysuckle, and awoke the next morning determined to find Hooker's journals.

I had little to go on. I knew Hooker Hopkins was one of the three children of the last marriage of Elisha Hopkins. There may have been others, but the census records listed only those three and no one ever mentioned any others. I called my mother in Tennessee the next morning to ask her what she knew about Hooker. To escape over fifty years of memories of my father in their tiny home on Greasy Creek, she had moved in with my sister in Murfreesboro, where John Cabell Breckinridge led his Kentucky Orphan Brigade into history at the Battle of Stones River.

"Sary Ann was his wife's name," she said, using the mountain diminutive for Sarah. "I believe Hooker died and I guess they both are. They had a boy named Ersel, but I don't know if he's living or not." *Sarah Ann* rang a bell. In my research, I had come across a child named Otra Hopkins who died in 1918, three days after birth. Her mother's maiden name was Sarah Ann Sparkman. Could this have been one of their children?

"How old would Ersel be?" I asked my mother.

"He must be pretty old," she said. "He was older than Marvin." Dad was born in 1922. I began to pray Ersel was still alive.

"Do you remember where they lived, Mom?"

"Down in Floyd County is all I know. Marvin and I used to go see them sometimes. I believed they lived on Beaver Creek or somewhere."

"Do you remember if they ever had a daughter named Otra?"

"No, I don't know any child they had besides Ersel."

"Well, I found a Hopkins child who died in 1918 whose mother was a Sarah Ann Sparkman."

"*Sary Ann*," she said again. "That was her name. I don't know if she was a Sparkman."

"There was another girl born to Sarah Ann. Her name was Virginia, she was born in 1920, but I couldn't find any death date for her. Did you know anything about her?"

"No, I just knew Ersel."

We chatted a while longer. Eventually I told her I loved her and hung up. She needed her rest, and she had her own hauntings to deal with.

I went to the computer and began searching Floyd County records for Sarah Ann Sparkman. I found her in Knott County, which borders Floyd and Pike, on a Sparkman family webpage. She was indeed the wife of Hooker Hopkins and had died in 1972. The page listed a son named Hershell, which I assumed to be a corruption of Ersel, but did not give a date of death for either Hooker or Ersel.

Later that week, I went to the library to research the obituaries from 1972 and I found Sarah Ann's. According to the obit, only her son, Ersel, survived her. Hooker had died in 1959. *The same year his brother died, I thought.* The funeral arrangements were by the Merion Funeral Home, which I knew had gone out of business after the owner died. Ironically, the owner, Paul Merion, had been a friend of my father's. There was a Merion Monument Company still in business, and the next day I called them.

Indeed, Paul's son owned the company, and he gave me some directions to the cemetery, but said he no longer had any of his father's records. They were lost in one of the floods that periodically ravaged the Big Sandy Valley.

The cemetery was in Knott County, just over the Floyd county line from Lackey, where Hooker and Sarah Ann had lived. He suggested I contact another funeral home in Knott

County for better directions and I did. Their directions were better, although still somewhat vague. But with the hope that someone near the cemetery would be able to finally direct me, I struck out for Knott County the following weekend.

In the summer foliage, the cemetery was not visible from the road. In fact, I never found it, and as I learned later, I would not have been able to reach it anyway for it was across a swollen creek and the bridge was washed out. However, after knocking on the first door I came to, I met Sarah Ann's niece who treated me like kinfolk when I introduced myself. She told me that Hooker and Sarah Ann were both buried on the now-inaccessible cemetery, and, to my obvious disappointment, Ersel was dead.

Do you know anything about any journals Hooker had?" I asked her.

"No,' she said, "but there was a Collins lady Ersel used to work for who might help. You should also see my nephew, and he'll take you to the cemetery."

I went to her nephew's house, but there was no one home. A neighbor wandered by and told me where the cemetery was located, and he told me about the washed-out bridge. I went back to Floyd County to find Mrs. Collins.

Beulah Collins was retired, and she lived in a comfortable home in sight of the business she used to run. I knocked on the door and she invited me in.

Yes, she remembered Ersel very well; he worked for her after he sobered up. *Sobered up?*

"Did he drink?" I asked.

"Not before he went into the service," she said. "But he stayed drunk for twelve years after he came back."

Sarah Ann also used to clean house for her, she told me.

"Do you know anything about any journals Hooker may have left?" I asked.

She thought for a minute, as if the question rang some long-silent bell. "No, I don't think so, but you ought to ask Buster Ramey about them. Ersel lived with them before he died."

I asked her who was 'them?' "Was it Buster and his wife?"

"No, Buster's wife's dead. He lives with his sister."

"Where do they live?" I asked.

She lifted an arm to point to a window in her living room. Straight across the street, she told me, and I began to prepare for next interview.

Before I left, I asked Mrs. Collins to tell me about Hooker. I had heard he was a very courteous man, and I wondered if that was her recollection.

"He was polite," she agreed, "but he could still cuss. I never got a cussin' like he gave me one time."

"What was that about?"

"When I had the store, canned biscuits had just come out and Hooker bought a can for breakfast. He just put them up on the mantle above the stove and the next morning they had blown up. Had dough all over the place. He cussed me 'til a fly wouldn't light on me." She laughed somewhat painfully and then said: "I gave him his money back anyway." Apparently, Hooker was his father's son.

I thanked Mrs. Collins for her help and went outside, pausing on her front porch to prepare my speech. Across the narrow road of the old coal camp I could easily see the home of Buster Ramey. *Are those journals somewhere in that old weathered house, I wondered?* My heart quickened as I stepped off Beulah Collins' porch for the final leg of my journey.

Buster Ramey and his sister Cora lived in an old mining camp house slowly disintegrating from the accumulated settlement of moss and coal dust on its sagging roof and the usual lack of care afforded to the home of someone no longer able to maintain it. An old Chevrolet pickup truck with a camper top, covered with a creeping layer of mold, was parked in front of the house, almost against the dilapidated porch, as if placed there to prop up the house in case it should slip off its underpinnings. I assumed it belonged to Mr. Ramey as well. Mrs. Collins had told me Buster and his sister were very suspicious, and may not talk to me, but I had hope as I climbed the sagging steps of their porch, trying to form the words in my mind that I wanted to say.

I knew I was closing in on the journals, and I wanted to do nothing that would spook him. Mrs. Collins had also said that both Buster and his sister needed to be in a nursing home, but they were afraid of losing what little money they had accumulated over the years, and they did not trust strangers because such people always tried to do things for them. Apparently, they were not accustomed to having things done for them.

I screwed up my courage and knocked on the door. A kindly, white-haired gentleman with a short, spiky white beard came to the door.

"Mr. Ramey? I'm Ersel Hopkins' cousin. Could I speak to you about him?"

He pushed open the door and stepped back. He looked at me up and down.

"Come on in," he said. "I knew it was you soon I saw you."

You know me, I wondered? I've never seen you before in my life.

Wesley Ramey, better known as Buster, lived with his sister alone in the house where they grew up. After both their spouses died, the siblings had moved in together. Buster attempted to take care of his sister as best he could for a man approaching eighty. Though his sister was younger, her health was poorer. She was blind and her feet and legs were swollen, the result of diabetes that had wrested the vitality from her and was slowly claiming her life. She was sitting in a chair next to the kitchen table when I entered, and I suspected most of her life was now centered around that table.

Buster extended his hand and I took it. There was little strength in it, but it was not feeble; it was gentle, made so by years of tending to his invalid sister.

"My real name is Wes," he said. "But you can call me Buster, everybody else does. My sister's Cora; Cora Reed. I knew you was a Hopkins."

But how, I wondered? I shared none of the usual Hopkins physiognomy.

We sat in rickety chairs next to the table and talked softly as Cora slept. After a while, he pointed out her swollen feet, now red and peeling.

"That's called edema," I said. "It's usually associated with a heart condition. Has she been to the doctor lately?"

"Yeah," he said. "That's what the doctor said." She woke up after that and Buster introduced me to her.

"Cora? This is Bruce Hopkins, Cora. He's Ersel's cousin."

In her darkness, she extended her hand. It was tiny and softened from her years away from the kitchen. I wondered how many meals that hand had prepared before she became an invalid. We chatted for a minute or so, before she startled me with a question.

"Are you a Christian, Bruce?" she asked.

"Yes, Ma'am, I am," I told her immediately. I was surprised at the suddenness of her question, and my view of religion might not have fully meshed with hers, but I gave her the answer I thought she expected. Indeed, I still seethed over the Old Regulars' abandonment of my father the night of his wake, but I had no interest in a theological discussion now. I would not have upset her for the world and I suppressed whatever defense I could have offered of my views of religion for her sake.

"Well, it's a good idea to have some kind of insurance," she said. *Well, I thought, maybe my view of religion was not that far removed from hers.* We went on to talk about Hooker and his family.

"Ersel lived with us until he died," Buster said. "That was about ten years ago. He was my cousin. His mother was our mother's sister."

That pleased me. At least, Ersel had some family to come home to before he died, but I wondered if they would be defensive about the next question I had.

"Mrs. Collins said Ersel drank after he came back from the service. Is that true?" I asked.

"Yeah, he was drunk for about ten or twelve years. Stayed in his room at Hooker's house. He had a pension from the Army. He got hurt, you know."

"I didn't know that," I said. "I didn't know Ersel very well."

"He was a good boy," Buster said. "Let me show you a picture of him." And he retreated to a corner of the room to bring back a round metal frame with an American eagle spread above Ersel's picture.

"That's all we have left of him," he said.

I studied the picture. It had probably been taken after boot camp. His hair was still short and there was no insignia of rank on his sleeve. He was smiling and there was a knowing upturn to the corner of his lips. His hat was cocked a little to one side, in the style popular among American soldiers during World War II. He did resemble me.

"I got this, too," he said, showing me a laminated copy of Sarah Ann's obituary.

"I was just a kid when I knew Ersel," I said. "Everybody looked big then. Was he a big man?"

"Pretty big," Buster said. "He was a little shorter than you, but he was taller than Hooker." He leveled his palm at about his Adam's apple to indicate Hooker's height.

"Mr. Ramey, what I'm interested in is knowing what might have become of some journals Hooker had," I said. I went on to explain how Hooker had visited the Old Prater Cemetery and had written about it in journals at night, and how I needed those journals to help me identify the remaining unknown graves on the cemetery.

"I wonder if Hooker may have left those journals for Ersel, and if Ersel may have left them with you."

"Nope," Buster said. "Ersel didn't leave nothin', 'cause he didn't have nothin' to leave. About a year after Hooker died, the flood took their house down the river. It came up so fast they lost everything. That's when Sarah Ann came to live with us. She was our aunt, and we were the only family she had left."

Down the river? Gone? Everything gone?

I was dumbstruck. Again, the very tools I needed for my work were denied me, snatched away before I could ever touch them, let alone read them. My mouth was suddenly dry, but I managed to croak another question: "Did you ever see Hooker's journals?"

"Nope," Buster said. "I remember that big ol' leather bag, but I don't guess he told nobody much of what was in there."

So there was nothing for me. There would be no magic valise where all my questions had their answers. Again, I mentally kicked myself for not beginning this project sooner, before there was any thought of rebuilding 460, and before my neglect of my family would reach beyond the pale. Although I had no hopes of finding any new information on the cemetery, perhaps there would be something I could learn about Hooker and his family.

"Is Ersel buried with Hooker and Sarah Ann?" I asked.

"Nope," Buster said. "Ersel's buried out here on the city cemetery. They call it the Chapman cemetery, but it's really the city cemetery. The two girls are buried with them."

"Was that Otra and Virginia?" I asked.

"No, it was Virginny and Arizony," Cora said. She used the diminutive now where she had not used it with Sarah Ann.

"Arizona?" I asked. "I didn't know they had an Arizona."

"There was another boy, too, I think," she said. "His name might have been Clinard, but I'm not sure. They all died young, though. Those little girls were beautiful; they had that beautiful blond hair. Ersel was the only child to grow up."

"Is Otra buried with Sarah Ann and Hooker?" I asked.

"No," Buster said. "That's the one they left in Pike County. She's buried on Greasy Creek, I reckon, but I don't know where. I went up there with Ersel, but we couldn't find it. I've been to all their graves but hers."

"Was it the Old Prater cemetery you visited?" I asked.

"I believe it was," he said. "It was up on a hill."

Things were falling into place now. Hooker and Sarah Ann had at least two other children besides Otra and Ersel and they both died as children. Otra was buried on the Old Prater

84

Cemetery, but there was no stone, and her name was not on the cemetery list. Was that the reason Hooker was on the cemetery back in the Fifties? Was he looking for his child's grave?

"And Ersel never married?" I asked.

"No," he said. "He never had a girlfriend after he came back from the war. He never sung anymore either."

"He was a singer?" I asked.

"Yeah, he was a good one. He could sing anything you wanted to hear, but he never sung a song after he came back."

"From the war?"

"Yeah."

"And he had a pension?"

"Yeah."

"Then he must have had some kind of injury that…uh…that prevented him from ever having children," I offered.

"That's what I figured," Buster said. "He never did say anything about it, and I didn't ask. You know him and Sarah Ann both lived with us before they died. This was about the only home they had."

His eyes focused on nothing in particular in the darkening house, except for glancing at the ghosts of his boyhood rustling past him.

"I miss him a lot," he said.

The pieces were snapping into place like a child's puzzle. Ersel was born in 1915, Otra was born in 1918, and Virginia was born in 1920. There may have been children in between. There was also Arizona, probably born sometime in the early Twenties, and maybe one other child. None, except Ersel, survived childhood.

Hooker and Sarah Ann moved to Floyd County not long after Virginia was born, and probably neglected Otra's grave. It is difficult to fault them; three days of life offer little opportunity to beget memories. Otra may have had a wooden marker for her grave, but it would have been claimed by the elements long ago. Or she may have had a simple fieldstone that eventually rolled away or no marker at all. Many graves were never marked, and acknowledged only by yearly scraping of the undergrowth and mounding of the grave to make it appear fresh and new, as if the funeral had just taken place. At one time on Greasy Creek, only the memories of the living marked the graves.

There were other possibilities. Perhaps the Spanish Influenza epidemic of 1918 took the life of the gravedigger, making it even more difficult for Hooker find where his child was buried. By the 1950's, it would have been obvious to Hooker that Ersel could not have children and it would have been too late for Hooker and Sarah Ann. *It was clear to me now what he was doing on the cemetery: he was trying to find the lost grave of his child so he could mark it before his own death.*

Cora was getting tired, and I wanted to make my exit while she was still awake so I could tell her goodbye. When I said I had to go, she clutched my hand and looked at me with sightless eyes.

"Thank you for coming to see us. You'll come back, won't you?" she pleaded. "Nobody every comes around here anymore."

"I'll be back," I said. "I promise."

I shook hands with Mr. Ramey and went out the door. The sun was down, and the last of the light was retreating after it. I pulled on my headlights as I drove back to Pike County and thought about my day. I did not have what I had come for, and I had only one new piece of information about the Old Prater: that there was another unknown grave somewhere on that hill. But it had been a good day. And I had brought a little bit of light into an old woman's dark world and I had brought back the ghost of a cousin and friend for one last visit with a lonely old man.

Later that summer, on another visit to Ohio to visit Aunt Bessie, I asked Caudill about his cousin Ersel. His eyes lit up when he spoke of him. Caudill said Ersel had one of the best singing voices he ever heard, and that he had more women than anybody he ever knew.

Ersel would often come back to Greasy Creek to stay with Big Will, and he would collect the boys of the creek in his car and they would go out to drink and chase women. Ersel was almost an icon to those boys who were looking for heroes in the sad world of the coal camps, but it was his singing that Caudill remembered so well.

"He was singing at one of those roadhouses once," Caudill said. "And after he finished he came back over to our table. I was just a kid, but Ersel got me in. There I was: fifteen years old and drinking a beer. I thought I was on top of the world.

"There was another old boy there who came over to our table. He said, 'Ersel, God damn it, I been looking all over hell and gone to find that record you were singing last weekend. What was it, anyway?' 'Hell,' Ersel said. 'That ain't no record. I just made it up.' And he laughed."

Caudill smiled, remembering one of his boyhood heroes in his greatest glory.

"He sure could sing," he said.

Hooker Hopkins, perhaps named for a Union general in a Confederate cavalry song, was born in 1884 and died in 1959, not long after his older brother. In the last decade of his life, with all but one of his children dead in their youth, and that remaining child to remain forever childless, he came back to the Old Prater Cemetery. He came to find the grave of his daughter, whose life extended to only three days, and he never found it. Instead, he turned to the graves of his family, those graves he could still find, and he wrote down their stories in journals that were claimed by a flood. Perhaps he let Sarah Ann read them, or perhaps he kept them to himself and no one but he ever viewed what he wrote. And no one would.

For eighty years, Otra's grave has been lost and will probably remain lost forever. If a father cannot find his child's grave, no one else can, but in compensation, it can be said he tried.

It is not difficult to invoke an image of Hooker on that cemetery. I see him opening the gate and slipping quietly inside, so as not to disturb the souls gathering near him in the twilight. I see him writing in his journals, attempting to make permanent the stories that will be, like his daughter's grave, forever lost if he doesn't. *Was it because by doing so he would somehow expiate the guilt he felt for leaving some part of himself there?*

I can see him working into the night, until exhaustion overtakes him, then rolling out a blanket to rest until morning. I could also see myself, down in the valley looking up to see the light go out on the cemetery, and trembling from fear that some wraith had seen me and taken flight to my bedpost. I could see myself rushing back to my bed in my grandfather's house, and pulling up the covers to shut out the fiends that might have followed the beam of Hooker's lamp.

I often wonder where Hooker slept those nights he stayed on the cemetery. Perhaps next to Harrison, the nephew who became the closest thing to a father he ever knew, or between Harrison's grave and Lila's, where pink roses once grew, and it is not difficult to see him intoxicated by their fragrance, drinking it in as sleep claimed him.

Perhaps he lay on the ground where Cornelius and Dorcus were sleeping, inside the fence that had rusted into nothingness by the time I remembered it. Perhaps he thought his daughter might be buried there. Perhaps there were two or three such places and he lay here or there on different trips, in the hope that somehow he would be able to reach her and beg her forgiveness. Perhaps, perhaps, perhaps; I still did not know for sure. I was confident of nothing more than what I had been told, and I had been told little. Hooker's journals would have told me, but they were gone.

But I had seen his light. I know he was there on those nights, pressed against the earth, pleading for knowledge and direction, and I know that my vision, regardless of whence it comes, is not far removed from the truth:

He puts out his lamp and lies in the darkness, feeling the night envelop him like my grandmother's blankets once draped over my frail shoulders. Before he yields to sleep, he invokes the spirits of his ancestors to help him in the hope the tiny shade of his daughter will hear his heart beating, and will somehow be comforted in the knowledge that her father had not forgotten her after all.

And I can hear his prayer that she will, in the sublime reparation of the grave, forgive him his abandonment of her last plot of earth.

Elisha

In the spring of 2000, my brother and I decided to climb Ripley Knob, the hill that overlooks what is left of the old Greasy Creek camp, and on whose brow is the final resting-place of Elisha Hopkins. Neither of us had been there in decades and we intended to visit the little cemetery, which supposedly had five to seven graves, including Uncle Will's. We wanted to see if there were any tombstones and any discernible names or dates to help eliminate whom might be buried on the Old Prater.

According to a local genealogy, Elisha's first wife, Phoebe, our great-great-great grandmother, was buried with Elisha, but there was no mention of Mary, his last wife and Will's mother. Before 1911, Kentucky did not have a statewide system of vital statistics, so I did not know when Phoebe died. I last found her in the 1880 census, but I could not find her in 1900 or 1910. Practically the entire 1890 national census had been lost in a fire in Washington, so I could surmise she had died between 1880 and 1900. I knew Phoebe was gone before Elisha, but no one knew when. Mary outlived Elisha, and I traced her to Floyd County through 1920. A death certificate indicated she died a few years later but did not indicate where she was buried.

I had neglected to ask Buster Ramey about Mary when I was in Floyd County, but I suspect she was buried there. I did not believe she was buried on Ripley Knob, but Paul and I wanted to make sure. No one in the family in Pike County knew where she was buried, although her sister Lila, Harrison's wife, was buried on the Old Prater. There was the possibility she was among the unknowns there, but I did not think so. By now, with all my research as done as it could be, I was relying on instinct, or some ghostly communication to guide me and my spirits were telling me she was buried somewhere else.

There were other reasons as well for our trip. It would be an opportunity for my brother and me, now in our 50's, to play like children again and tramp in the woods. It was also an opportunity for me to touch some tangible part of Elisha, even if it were only his gravestone. I had been scouring my paltry memory to attempt to recollect anything that referred to him, and odd things were happening. It was as if he were somewhere nearby, like a mischievous imp, now devoted to tormenting me, teasing me with odd flashes of scenes from long ago, scenes that came and went in a blink, but were somehow unsettlingly clear and vivid. I wanted to see if going to Elisha's grave would improve that channel of communication, if it were a channel, and not some fantasy I had created to assuage the guilt I felt for forty years of rejecting my ancestors.

Before he died, Will had made it clear to everyone he wanted to be buried "beside his mother and father," implying Mary was indeed buried on Ripley Knob. But that was supposedly what Rissie said, and perhaps she did not say "mother and father," perhaps she said only "father." Unfortunately, no one I talked to had a memory any clearer than my own, and I could find no confirmation of who was buried on Ripley Knob.

When Will died, my grandmother made the men of the creek take his body up the arduous road, or what was left of it, to one of the most inaccessible places on Greasy Creek to be buried in accordance with his wishes. She did this because she loved Will and not because she loved Elisha. Although Will was only her cousin, he had been taken in by her father as a son when his own father died. This was common in mountain families, and made genealogical research fitful.

Although fully grown when he entered Harrison's family, Will became the strong and kind older brother to all of Harrison's children and earned the respect the family accorded him even unto his death. And of course, no one on Greasy Creek would deny Rissie anything she wanted anyway; there were simply too many debts of love owed her for anyone to refuse such a small repayment.

As we climbed into my Jeep at my mother's house, my brother and I went over what I had learned in my research on the Hopkins family. Neither he nor I had placed any early emphasis on Elisha. When I first began my work, he was just a name attached to a caricature; I felt he had no real connection to me, especially since the patriarchal bond had been broken when his daughter had my great-grandfather illegitimately. But then I found out Elisha was Uncle Will's father! "Cripple Will," as some people unkindly called him, the old uncle who had been so kind to me, was the son of my great-great-great grandfather!

The Hopkins family was confusing enough to begin with, but when one of the patriarchs extended his reach across several generations, it was even worse. Furthermore, Elisha's last wife was his grandson's sister-in-law! How often did that occur in genealogies? By the time my brother and I began our climb to Elisha's tiny cemetery, I had fully realized that Elisha was not just a name on a roll of names from a dusty genealogy, but was almost close enough for me to touch. Indeed, I had touched his son, who used to embrace me with ancient, trembling arms when he would see me on the way to or from school.

"You remind me of your daddy, when he was a little boy," he would say.

For years, Uncle Will ran a store at the mouth of a little hollow just down the road from where I grew up. Behind the store was the house where he raised his family. In the early 1950's, when age was overtaking him, his two living children came down from Indiana to take him and Martha Ellen, his wife, back with them. Will refused, but allowed Martha Ellen to go.

"I can't take care of her," he said. "But I can't leave Greasy."

He was born here and he would die here, he told them. It broke his heart when she left and he closed the store he had opened with Elisha's inheritance.

Will was 34 when he married Martha Ellen Damron, who was 17. He had married late and she had married young, but their marriage was happy. Somewhere, on the Old Prater, or perhaps on the mountaintop where Elisha was buried, or somewhere else, that gravesite also lost in history, was their first child, a daughter. I do not know if that was the reason he stayed, but he did, and after Parkinson's Disease prevented him living alone, he moved in with Rissie to die. It was to her house that he retreated, where Rissie could help feed him when he could no longer hold a fork, although he would walk the road that was once the railroad track from the Greasy Creek camp to Andrew Prater's store almost every day.

Many times I would look up from my lessons at the Middle Greasy schoolhouse to see Uncle Will, tall, gaunt and now stooped, painfully retracing his steps from Rissie's house to Andrew's store to assume his place behind the coal stove with the elders of Greasy Creek.

When Rissie and Harlen married, they first moved in with Harrison, as did Frank and Ethel, but as her younger sisters grew able to take care of their father, Rissie wanted a place of her own. Will gave them a spot on Ripley Knob where they built a small house until they could afford a larger one and acquire more land for farming. Just above them lived Harlen's father, Jack Damron, who was also Martha Ellen's father. I once asked my father, as we drove by the mountain, if he had any pets when he was a boy.

"Yep," he said. "I had two dogs: Farley and Jack. Named the last one after Jack Damron. He gave him to me."

Dad was surprised at the rush of memory, and he thought for a minute before going on. It was the last year of his life, and the diabetes that was ravaging his body had also strained his ability to think, but that image of his childhood came back as clear and resonant as a church bell.

"Boy, what do you know about that?" he said. "It just all came back to me."

I saw him smile as he remembered his dogs and the loyalty they must have shown him when he came home from school and they tumbled down the mountain toward their young master.

"What was it like then, Pop, to live up there?" I asked.

"It was good. I used to help Uncle Will sometimes in the store and around the house," he said with perfect clarity. "Marthy Ellen used to bake pies and leave them on the windowsill to cool. They'd smell so good it'd drive me crazy. We didn't have much to eat then and it would tickle me to death when Marthy Ellen would send a pie home with me."

There was nothing left of his childhood now in that hollow. The little houses on the flats were all gone, as was Will's house and the store. After years of abandonment, the old house fell in and the pranksters of the creek burned the store to the ground one Halloween.

I had often asked my family about Uncle Will and how he related to our family. Obviously, he was a Hopkins, but how was he an uncle? He was not my grandmother's brother, yet he was just as close and, just as obviously, loved. When I asked these questions, I never got a clear answer. It was as if the attempt to explain his genealogy was too complicated for words.

If the paternal genealogy was confusing, it was just as difficult to unravel the maternal side. Not only was Will the son of Rissie's great-grandfather, he was also the son of her aunt. Elisha had married Mary Riley in 1878, when he was 67 and she was 22, according to the marriage license. My calculations showed her closer to 13. Harrison, Elisha's grandson, later married her younger sister Delilafare, whom the family remembered as just "Lila." Mary, also known as Polly in the vernacular of the time, was his last wife, and the mother of his fourth family. He had married Phoebe and had his first family, and had two other families before Mary came along.

In 1860, Elisha had three families living beside each other at the forks of Greasy Creek. One was Phoebe and her brood, and to either side was another woman and hers. One was Sarah Robinson, known as Sally, who gave him his first family outside of marriage and the other was Mahala Blackburn, known as Haley, who gave him his second.

In 1877 Phoebe sued Elisha for abandonment after he moved to another part of the county with Haley when she became ill. Haley later died, and Elisha stayed on, alone in the cabin he had built for her, away from his wives and children, going quietly insane until Phoebe pulled him back to reality with her lawsuit. By 1878, now divorced and with his senses restored, Elisha was ready for another woman; that was Mary, who was just a child, and who brought back something of the youth he had lost with Haley's death.

Even though Phoebe divorced Elisha, she still lived with him. Apparently, it was not that easy to give up Elisha Hopkins. In the 1880 census Phoebe is listed in his household as his "widowed sister." A joke on the census taker perhaps, but maybe he still wanted Phoebe around. Anything having to do with Elisha was always complicated. And he was never called Elisha.

He was always "Lige," or, more properly, "Ol' Lige." The last census entries before his death list him as "Lige," as he preferred. Even today, there are people living on the creek who were accused, after an episode of exhibiting some particularly stubborn or cantankerous behavior, or using some especially profane language, as being "just like Ol' Lige Hopkins." That alone was usually enough to reform the most Procrustean nature of the accused.

Elisha was still a legend among the old folks on the creek, even though there was no one still alive who knew him, or had the mental faculties to describe him when I began my work on the Old Prater. My grandmother Lexie Prater would have remembered, but a series of strokes had enfeebled her by the time I began my quest. It was another incident of my trying to get on board a moment after the boat had gone. My great aunt Bessie Robinson was in diapers when Elisha died, and she could tell me stories, but could not describe the man.

I had so many questions and no answers. Was he short? Was he tall? Was he dark complexioned or fair? Did he have a beard or was he clean-shaven? What was his voice like? I knew he had been born a generation after the Revolution, and had lived into the 20th Century. Did he keep the mannerisms of Old Virginia when he came to Kentucky? Was he just an anachronism and misunderstood by a race that he no longer represented?

I wanted to know these things because I had always wondered where my genes came from. I was tall and dark, while the Hopkins, at least most of them, were short and fair, except for Uncle Will, who was also tall. When I knew him, his hair was white. Was Elisha tall? In 1890, his son George W. applied for a soldier's pension and was described as 50 years old, with black hair and black eyes. His height was listed as 5'11". My hair used to be black, and my eyes still are, and I am still 6'2". I had assumed those genes came from the Prater side of the family, but could they have been some residual DNA from Ol' Lige finally showing up in me? By contrast, my brother was shorter, and the family delighted in calling him Little Harrison, in honor of our great-grandfather. But whose genes had we inherited?

We could not have determined any of this, of course, from merely visiting Elisha's grave. I had been there only a few times in my youth, while squirrel hunting or just roaming the hills, and I had never been there as an adult. I wanted to go back to see if there was any message waiting for me on that windy mountaintop. My brother and I wanted to see if there were any clues that would help us unravel the mysteries of the Old Prater, and we both wondered why Elisha would have picked such a remote place to be buried.

There are no photographs of Elisha, at least none I have been privy to, nor are there photographs of any of his women, although there had been photographs of Mary. Unfortunately, the river that claimed his journals also claimed Hooker's family pictures, and if Uncle Will's children had any, they were gone, too. Mink and her brother Victor, like so many sons and daughters of Greasy Creek, moved away. I remember only Mink and her irrepressible warmth, and I knew practically none of their children. Except for a hazy memory of Mink's daughter, a shy, beautiful little girl, I would not know them if they met me on the mountaintop.

Since there were no photographs, I created images for Elisha's women in my mind. I had no image for Mary, however, and I suspected this was because I knew that I would somehow find a picture of her and her ghost would have no reason to project an image to me. Phoebe, Sally and Haley were all gone, and I knew there would be no photographs ever to appear of them. I could feel safe in my creations.

Quantitatively, I tried to add or subtract certain physical features from Elisha's descendants, using certain commonalties among them and produce a composite of Elisha as a result. I could not do it, but from the process, I could deduce that Dorcus' children were somewhat short because her lover was. Harmon's children were even shorter. However, my grand-mother Laura, who married my grandfather after he returned from madness, was taller and big-boned. She was the daughter of Daniel Albert Blackburn, the son of Elisha and Haley. Perhaps her size had something to do with Haley's genes. Uncle Will, Mary's child, was tall and big-boned, but his brother Hooker was short and delicate. But Mary and Lila were sisters, and Lila's children were small like Hooker. Perhaps Elisha's DNA was overpowered by his wives', except, perhaps, for Uncle Will. Maybe that was why Will was so determined to return to his father's side. Maybe Elisha was especially good to him because Will was closest in size to himself and perhaps doted on him.

No matter how hard I tried, it was impossible to create a picture of Lige, but I could somehow picture his women. There were phantom images that came to me, based more on their spirits than on their flesh and I somehow felt I knew them. I could at least place them chronologically.

Phoebe Adkins was his first love, and was perhaps a woman before he became a man, although I sensed they were both young and inexperienced, and if any physical flaws existed in Phoebe, Elisha overlooked them in his early passion. I do not see her as tall as Elisha, even though their son George probably was. Phoebe's brother Jesse married Elisha's sister Elizabeth at about the same time, and with the loneliness of the Adkins and Hopkins families in the wilderness of Greasy Creek of 1833, the marriages may have been as much political as passionate.

Two years later Elizabeth died, and in 1837 Jesse married again. Her grave was probably among those obliterated before Jim Prater ran his hogs over the lower cemetery. It may have been her early death, probably in childbirth, that gave Elisha the philosophy that life is short and should be lived to the fullest, a philosophy he practiced for another lifetime.

But I could not envision him not loving Phoebe, even if I can sense his restlessness. I can see the years passing, her body growing heavy as she settles into the routines of domestic life and Elisha's sexual spirit, now awakened by his cognizance of the women available to him, is ignited.

The next, Sally Robinson, was probably his first love outside of marriage. I suspect she was the shortest of Lige's women, again because of her children. I see her as having a dark, gypsy-like beauty, somehow exotic to Elisha, perhaps bewitching, as if she had the younger, petite qualities of Phoebe, but somehow made more intense, even more than the contrast of her youth would allow. There is something otherworldly in her image, as if she were privy to secrets only Indian women had, passed on from mother to daughter in secret, by the light of the full moon perhaps, at certain times as the stars allowed it. No one had proof of her ancestry, but everything pointed to her as the daughter of Samuel Robinson who married Elisha's sister Matilda in 1867. No one had any information on Samuel's first wife, but I had a notion.

Samuel came from Russell County, Virginia, probably to live with relatives in Pike County, but he most likely came to Russell County from North Carolina. The first Robinsons in Pike County came here from North Carolina, escaping the persecution afforded Cherokees on their ancestral lands since the country was formed. When President Jackson moved the Civilized Tribes away from the rich lands they owned into the American interior, it was supposedly to reduce conflict with the burgeoning nation surrounding them. Many Cherokees disappeared from the great trek to Oklahoma they were ordered to undertake in 1838, and I suspect Samuel was one of those who escaped, but could not keep his wife with him. He had only his daughter Sarah when he came here, probably because he could have hidden or carried her easily. Sarah, known as Sally to all her descendants, was a small woman and must have been a small child when Samuel excused himself from the nineteenth-century concentration camp in the unknown American West offered him by the government.

Perhaps he wanted freedom for himself and for his daughter, or perhaps Sally was the only one he could steal without detection from the US Army, which was herding the Cherokee. Only when he received final word that his first wife was dead would he marry Matilda, by whom he had several children. When they married, he was 73 and she was 49.

Elisha was probably Sally's first love, and became the mother of his second family. She remained true to him long after he began a third.

Haley was his third consort, and she was physically different from both Phoebe and Sally. Perhaps Mahala Blackburn Cassady was a challenge for Elisha, but he won her, taking her away from her husband and two children. She must have been vibrant, spirited, probably a larger woman than Phoebe or Sally, but shapely, with womanliness exuding from her in heated waves. Her hair is lighter than Phoebe's or Sally's, and she embodies the youth that he recognizes is slipping away from him.

At first she is the healthiest of Elisha's women, but after the War, her health begins to rapidly decline. It is of no concern at first, since everyone was emaciated from the scarcity of food, but she does not improve. Sensing her own death approaching, she seeks to return to her parents with her infirmity. *Or her guilt for leaving her children for Elisha.* But they will have nothing to do with her. He becomes more protective of her, more accommodating of her wishes, although he would never admit it, he falls more in love with her every day.

I learned that some of the Blackburns had suffered from a genetic kidney disease, still fatal to those acquiring it. Had that been what happened to Haley? And had his loss of her, combined with the loss of his beloved brother, caused the misanthropism of Elisha's final years? Whatever the case, she is the only one of his women not to live into old age, and I suspect he is never able to accept her loss. In the 1870 census, her children are living with Elisha's daughter Dorcus, who is beginning to assume the role of caretaker for three broken families.

Mary Riley was Elisha's last love, or at least his last wife. I suspect he loved her as much as he loved Phoebe or Sally, but he had not recovered from losing Haley when he married a child when he was already an old man. I suspect Mary always knew she would lose by comparison to Haley, but she was not part of the past. By the time he met her, Haley was gone and Elisha had begun to forget any of his life before the War. He is over sixty when he marries her and she barely in her teens. Perhaps he assumes he can recapture his youth with each succeeding youthful woman, and each time he takes a bride, he can start over. But although he lives another 31 years after this marriage, she is the one to outlive him. He has buried all his women except for Mary by the time he dies in 1909 and I do not expect her to be beside him on that hilltop. I suspect that of his women, only Phoebe and possibly Sally were buried in that isolated spot.

But for all his wild ways, Elisha had engendered the loyalty of his son, for Will chose to be buried by his father instead of his wife. Obviously, the man had an impact, but I had pitifully few tools to assess that now, having squandered the opportunities to learn more about my progenitor when I was younger, when the patriarchs and matriarchs of my family still lived. What I personally knew was little more than a half-remembered scattering of references by members of the family, usually accompanied by a shaking of the venerable head that uttered them. I had discovered much by pouring over old records in the county courthouse, and piecing together connections from those records, but I was still confused when it came to fixing an image of the man.

All I knew for certain was that he was buried on that mountaintop, and that there was a fieldstone with a name and a date that I assumed marked his grave. I had paid little attention to it when we buried Uncle Will, and I had paid no more attention to it when I would pass it on my childhood hunting trips. On those occasions, I would pause at his grave and weep for the kindly old man I had loved in my youth. So now, my brother and I were going back, to revisit the past and to attempt to pry loose some clues to the family mysteries.

We decided not to take the direct upland route this time. It was completely overgrown and very steep, even though it would have taken us past the places where Will had his store and his house, and where Rissie and Harlen had their first house, and where Jack Damron and his family lived. That road, if it still existed, was mostly vertical, and the latest owner of the property had bulldozed the old house and store sites anyway.

Also, Paul felt the trip would be too difficult. He had lost a lung to bronchiectasis in 1966 and had three abdominal hernia operations since then due to his constant coughing. In fact, neither of us was sure he could even make the trip. I had a contingency plan to return and complete the trip if my brother could not make it all the way. So we decided to take the more gradual route from the head of Big Bug Hollow about a mile down the road, the same route we took in 1959 when we carried Uncle Will to his rest.

Big Bug was where the mine foremen and their families lived when the Corrigan-McKinney Steel Company operated the Greasy Creek Mine. It was above the town where miners lived in sturdy two-story houses which were actually parallel apartments, two rooms downstairs and two rooms upstairs. Each apartment had its own well and outhouse. The company had the outhouses cleaned regularly by honeydippers.

"Honeydippers" was a derisive term used to describe the men employed to scoop out privies. The miners thought such work beneath them, so the company always faced a shortage of honeydippers and paid them more than they paid the miners. One honeydipper waited just until the rate came up to the point he would do the work and accepted the job. He saved his money and when he accumulated enough, built one of the finest houses on Greasy Creek with its own electric power plant and rich wood paneling. When the mines closed, he retired in relative luxury while the rest of the miners found themselves in penury, and the cycle of out-migration from the coalfields began. His house still stands, on Snake Branch, just up the hollow from the house Rissie and Harlen built when they moved from Big Will's hollow, while most of the camp houses are long gone. My Aunt Ola, Avery's widow and herself a descendant of Samuel Robinson, still lives there, although the road project will soon take that house too.

The camp houses, built, owned, and maintained by the company, were crowded together, barely ten feet apart, enough to drive a team of mules through for repairs to the company-owned structures and to allow honey-dippers room to remove their cargo. But there was some space in back for small kitchen gardens for the families to raise beans and tomatoes. Concrete sidewalks created a military precision to the camp, and life was regimented and attune to the rhythms of the mine.

A large building known as the Greasy Creek Hotel stood in the middle of the town, and served as housing for the unmarried supervisors of the mine as well as accommodations for the occasional visitors from Pittsburgh or Cleveland. There was a company hospital, as well as a company school and a company church. On the edge of town was a baseball field supplied by the company for recreation, and on another edge was a movie theater owned by my great-grandfather Luke Hamlin, Lexie's father. The company allowed a certain amount of free enterprise, and Luke capitalized on it.

My great-grandfather Peter Prater was the contractor who built the town. When the company executives came to Greasy Creek, they selected Peter because of his reputation for strength and honesty.

"All I asked them for was a good day's pay for a good day's work," he told me once. "That's what I asked the company and that's what I asked the men."

Paw Pete even fired his son Andrew, my grandfather, on two occasions because he felt Andrew was "not that partial to hard work." Everything built by Peter Prater was strong like him and intended to last. He was 101 when he died.

He also built the Big Bug houses, where company officials had conveniences the average worker could only dream of. There were bathrooms and running water in their houses, and the great steam generator that supplied power for the mine was tapped to ensure there would always be light for them to socialize by. They did not have to suffer with open hearths for heat; hot water boilers kept their quarters warm at night. But few miners begrudged them their luxuries. The company had made two things readily available that were previously in short supply: jobs and shelter. And in the grand new economy, the past, the past of Elisha Hopkins and the pioneers, became inconsequential.

Greasy Creek was a colony of the larger McKinney Steel operation at Wolfpit, just across the mountain from Greasy Creek. Overtaxed during World War I to supply the needs of the war economy, the company expanded after the war, and became the Corrigan-McKinney Steel Company when one of the partners died and his son came into power. The post-war economy boomed for a while, but by 1929, it was no longer viable to keep two separate operations on the same coal seam.

The Greasy Creek mine was closed, ending an era of unprecedented prosperity for the region.

It also ended an era of death and destruction unmatched since the Civil War. At any time, after the opening of the mine, one could see lines of jobless men outside the hiring office, waiting for someone to die in the mines so the next man on the list could take the place of the deceased. As coal towns go, Greasy Creek was not a bad place to live and work, but the specter of violent death in the mines was always present. It was as expected as nightfall.

Also on the edge of town were the occasional saloons where the men of the town would take some comfort from the stress of working in the mountain with death always at their shoulders. Not far away by rail was Pikeville, the county seat, where other pleasures could be had for a price, and the miners of Greasy Creek always had money, as long as they had the willingness to go into the pits. *Life is short, they would rationalize. Why can't we have a little fun before we go?*

Although the Greasy Creek mine did not shut down because of the Great Depression, the decline of the national economy prevented it from reopening. By 1940, the company had sold off the property to anyone with enough money to buy one of the houses or buildings where, for only a decade, a real town existed. One by one, the houses disappeared, and by the time my brother and I began our trek in 2000, there was little remaining of the booming community of eight decades before. There were only six original houses left in the camp, most redecorated to disguise the conformity of the old structures. The camp hospital was still standing, now a private home, with the family reporting the occasional odd thump or moan and attributing it to the ghosts of men who died there. A few houses, once the residences of the Big Bugs, were still standing, they too painted and newly-sided to cover their pasts. In the center of what was left of the town was the stately crumbling ruin of the Greasy Creek Hotel, its structure warped and sagging from termites and its windows smashed from rocks thrown by the urchins of the creek.

It was hard to believe that at one time there were over a hundred camp houses crowded into that small valley. The smooth concrete sidewalks had disappeared under the blacktop of later expansions of the roads and streets, and yards and gardens had returned to the plots where families once lived in quiet terror, awaiting a father or son to come home safe and alive for another day.

My brother and I looked down over the remnants of the town after we stopped and got out. We had driven as far as we could in four-wheel mode, and continued our journey on foot. We each carried bags with all the modern conveniences: a cell phone, bottled water, food packed in plastic or aluminum, and an electronic camera to take pictures on the way. I wondered aloud what the camp looked like before the mines came, when Elisha and his family owned most everything in sight.

"I don't know," my brother said. "But it would have to have been cleaner than it is today." My brother, as the Public Health Officer for Pike County, had sanitation as one of his gravest concerns. Back when the town was alive, the old privies were well maintained and leaching bacteria into the drinking water of nearby wells was not a problem in spite of their proximity. Today, open sewer lines from houses and incomplete underground septic systems made the streams dangerous, and the water table, destabilized by blasting from strip mines, could not clean the massive amount of effluent which too many people passed into it. E. Coli was always a problem, and finally the county laid water lines to replace the old wells that had faithfully served the people of Greasy Creek for generations. Now those wells were destroyed, and the people depended on county water, filled with chemicals, but at least germ-free, to sustain them.

The first part of the journey was uphill to the old tram road, which once connected the portals of the mine to the aerial tram. After getting there, we walked comfortably around the face of the mountain where other remnants of the physical operation of the coal mine stood, defying all efforts of nature to reclaim it. On the largest flat on the mountain, a great platform of concrete could still be seen. On this was built the upper tipple where the coal from the mine openings was dumped into a hopper, which, in turn, filled the tram baskets before sending them back down to fill waiting railroad cars.

A large building with walls of glass block once stood here. Known as the lamphouse, it was where the miner's battery lights were charged, awaiting pickup by the miners before they plunged into the darkness. Every day, the sun would reflect off those glass blocks into the town, as if it were a giant beacon, reminding the workers and their families that the mine was still there, and was the only reason for their existence.

My brother and I wondered what it was like to work in those pits as we made our way through the ruins. The mine entrance had a giant concrete façade with two portals with the words *Greasy Creek Mine, 1921,* above it. Both portals were closed; the mountain had fallen in on them. The narrow-gauge track that ran into the mine on one side, carrying in empty coal gondolas for the miners to fill was missing; Harlen removed it when the entire operation was being junked in 1940. After he completed that job, he went inside the mine where, after years of no maintenance, the roof collapsed on him.

How many men had walked into that mine through one portal, like Harlen, only to be carried out, bereft of limb or life, through the adjoining one? And what happened to their spirits, we silently wondered, when men died underground? Did the spirit follow the body outside, and wait for it to be returned to the earth for release? Or do the ghosts of men who met agonizing death under tons of rock still haunt those shafts, now sealed forever? Coal mines have always been battlegrounds, and battlegrounds are always haunted. I felt it in the air at Shiloh, or the Wilderness, and when I was at Gettysburg, a hundred years after the battle, the air was still thick with the unspeakable tragedy of those three days. A chill swept over both of us as we studied the old entrance, and we shivered before going on with our journey.

On the flat where batteries for the miners' lamps were charged, we stopped for lunch. The cell phone signal was clear at that elevation and we called back to let our families know we were OK. Without asking, I could sense the concern they had for Paul on this grueling climb. They should not have worried. Something propelled him up those nearly unmarked trails. He made the trip more easily than I had, and he rarely coughed during the journey. Afterwards, he said he had not felt that good in years, and had probably not felt that good when he was a child. *Life, I thought, has its small compensations.*

Paul gathered pieces of the tempered glass block from the lamphouse for souvenirs while I opened our bags to inspect our rations: pork-and-beans, mixed fruit, granola bars, fruit juice and aluminum cans of cola. We talked about Elisha while we ate, and after we finished, Paul gathered the litter from our meal to take back. We were not as conscious of the environment when we were younger, when sandwiches were wrapped in paper and pork-and-beans were still in tin cans. Everything that protected the food we ate that day would have been intact long after we were gone from this earth, and we did not want to further abuse the hillside. I noticed the rusting shape of a tin can near us, and I wondered if I tossed it there when I was still climbing these hills as a boy.

"You ever think of what it was like here, when the Hopkins first came to Greasy?" I asked my brother. "If Cornelius got a land grant, there must have been plenty of open land. There couldn't have been very many people living here."

"I've thought about it," he replied. "I just can't imagine Greasy Creek not being overcrowded with people."

Cornelius Hopkins came to Greasy Creek in 1822, when most of it was uninhabited. A hundred years later, when Marvin was born, the Greasy Creek mine was running and there were few flat places left for living. What land the coal camp had not taken was too remote to be of value, and people had learned to accommodate the mine. The prospect of the future was changed forever for Greasy Creek when the mines came, and that probably convinced Elisha that he had lived long enough. He died in 1909, as the speculators were buying up most of the coal rights.

From all indications, the Corrigan-McKinney Steel Company was more benevolent than most coal companies, in spite of almost constant fatalities. By the time the coal town era finally ended, sometime between the two world wars, relations between the miners and the coal companies were no longer congenial. In the 1950's the postwar depression had made armed camps of Pike County mines, which had largely escaped large-scale labor unrest like what happened in Pennsylvania or West Virginia. By the 1970's there were only a few large mines left in Pike County, with the coal companies dividing up their holdings into smaller "boundaries" to prevent union organization of their mines. The age of benevolence had passed.

Greasy Creek had always been depressing to me, but it was mostly a gentle place since the mine closed. It was difficult for me to image the clatter of the town in its heyday, let alone the pastoral beauty of the place before the coal mines came. I often wondered what Cornelius and his family thought when they saw their new home. Cornelius had come first in 1822; after building a homestead, he returned for his family in 1824 and said goodbye to Virginia. Elisha would have been about seven when his father left the first time, and was perhaps too young to plunge into the wilderness still traipsed by Indians. When the whole family set out, he would have been two years older, already a young man by the reckoning of the day. Would he have hidden behind his father's buckskin trousers, or would he have rushed ahead, leading the family at even that early age? I suspected the latter.

Elisha was not the only mountain patriarch with a small army of children; it was not that uncommon for a man with money to afford concubines. But there was still a code of conduct to be observed. My cousin Rex Hopkins once told me he was surprised when his father, Frank's brother Bud, told him that he once belonged to the Ku Klux Klan. He asked him, since there were few blacks in the mountains to persecute, why did he join the Klan? Mostly to make sorry fathers take care of their children, Uncle Bud told him. It didn't bother most mountain people that a man had children outside of wedlock;

most families had a few somewhere around, but it infuriated most mountaineers to see a man shirk the responsibility of taking care of his children. Apparently, the Klan served a rare humanitarian purpose in that instance.

Could Elisha have been a member of the Klan? He may have been a Grand Dragon for all I knew, but somehow I didn't think so. I suspect Elisha knew that nothing could have brought back his brother, and nothing could have brought back the life that existed before the War and he wanted no new battles that could never have changed the outcome of the old ones.

Perhaps he was prescient enough to see the future. Indeed, one of his children was supposedly able to cast spells and make chairs rock. Mary Wright had told me that when she was a child and had accompanied her mother to Harmon Robinson's house for dinner she saw with her own eyes what he could do.

Harmon lived in a rambling wooden house at the forks of Greasy Creek, in the middle of what was once Elisha's domain. It had been Sally's place, given to her by Elisha, and she gave it to their son Harmon when she died. When Mary, Harmon's wife, announced dinner and called him in from the front porch, the chair he had been sitting in followed him into the room.

"I'll never forget that," Mary said. "That little chair come right behind him like a pup. And nobody there thought anything at all about it. Harmon was just a'grinnin'"

My cousin Esther said Harmon's son Aaron also had that power and she had seen it too. By now, I could believe anything about Elisha and his families.

"He could make chairs rock by themselves," Esther said. "And he could call snakes and animals out of the woods. He would just cackle when he would do it, but he never tried to scare us with it."

Although I had never experienced any of the Robinson ability to levitate, I always wondered about the strange glint in Aaron's eyes or the crinkle of a smile that was always waiting at the corner of his lips. Did they get that power, if they indeed had it, from Sally? Would something reach out to me from Elisha's grave and tell me what I wanted to know? Would answers to the questions I had no earthly way of answering be somehow revealed to me on this trip?

Do ghosts appear in daylight?

After our break, we began the nearly vertical part of the trip to the flat where Jack Damron once lived. After the War a meetinghouse stood there, according to Mary Wright, where people from Greasy Creek and Hopkins Creek had church and dinners-on-the-ground. Hopkins Creek was a small tributary of the Big Sandy, just across the mountain from Greasy Creek and paralleling its larger sister. It was named for Elisha and his brother Joseph, who had the first land grants for the property. When Joseph sold his grant to Elisha and moved to Shelby Creek to raise cotton, Elisha became the master of Hopkins Creek as well. Now no one lived there, and only two small cemeteries admit to the place having served as home for generations of Hopkins' and Colemans. The mouth of the hollow is chained shut by a coal company gate.

I wondered why Elisha had started a church high up on that mountain, on the gap between the two creeks, if indeed he had: perhaps it was built later. Perhaps Will built it in his father's memory, but it was long gone. Only Mary Wright, of all my relatives, remembered it. Many of Elisha's contemporaries and most of his descendants were Old Regulars, but he was not on the Roll. I wondered if, after the War and after Joseph's death, he experimented with some other religion, or abandoned religion altogether. The Greasy Creek Regular Baptist Church was founded 38 years before he died, and his sister Matilda and his son Daniel Albert were among the first members. But I cannot find Elisha in the records of any church, including the Old Regulars and the Primitives, which both sprang from the flock that came together in 1871. I suspect that if he built the meetinghouse it had nothing to do with either denomination.

I grew up in the Old Regular Baptist Church, to which both the Praters and the Hopkins belonged, but I never felt comfortable there, or in any other church. Perhaps I had more of Elisha in me than I thought. There were indeed good people in the church, but I cannot yet forgive the others for walking out of my father's wake when the Masons arrived. I could understand why Elisha, with most of his children illegitimate in the eyes of the church, would not have been taken with their values.

Still, that did not answer the question of why Elisha built a meetinghouse on that gap. I concluded it was something else, something between the two brothers. Perhaps it was a memorial to his brother, placed in the spot where they played as children. Perhaps Hopkins Creek was their childhood playground. It is the next creek up the river from Greasy Creek, from Cornelius' land-grant homestead. Elisha and Joseph took land grants there in the 1850's, but soon afterward, Joseph went to Shelby Creek where the valley was wider and the soil richer. I sensed that Joseph was too restless to stay on Greasy or Hopkins Creek to make his living. I felt he wanted to do bigger things.

Bits and pieces of an ancient conversation began to form in my mind as we trudged up the hill. Each time I would pause to lean back against a tree, the words became clearer. By the time we arrived at the first flat, where somewhere Harlen and Rissie built their honeymoon cabin, the words were as clear as if I had heard them that morning:

"Tell me again, Joe. You want to do what?" Elisha asks his brother.

"Raise cotton," Joseph replies.

"This ain't Mississippi, brother. It's too cold to raise cotton."

"Nope, the government says you can raise cotton here. Just not as much."

"Aye, and if the government says angels will fly out of your ass, will you believe that too?"

Joseph merely smiles at his brother. He knows his brother will ultimately accept his argument. Elisha tries a different approach.

"Who's going to work it, brother? You got no niggers to pick cotton. How are you going to do that? You got to pay people to work."

"Me and Lucy and the children will do it, to start. Zach and Clary will take a share. I can offer shares to anyone who wants

to pick with us. I can find workers, brother. I just need property and you backing me."

Elisha knows his brother knows he will back him, he has always backed him, but he wants his brother to know the risk of borrowing money, especially against land. He wants to remind his brother of what happened to their father in 1819 when the banks closed and they wanted hard money from their customers for their debts. It did not matter that the banks would no longer take the money they themselves had printed. The notes were due, and much blood and sweat was all for naught as the foreclosures began. Elisha was only four, but he remembered the years of hardship and loss.

He is disappointed his brother does not want to continue farming here with him, but he knows Joseph would eventually want to find his own way. He is his brother, after all.

Indeed, there is the possibility he will make money. They had been to the meetings the government held in Pikeville to try to promote cotton growing in Pike County, and the arguments made sense. Since Pike County raised flax and shipped it to Cincinnati where it was made into bags, which were in turn shipped to New Orleans for baling cotton, it made sense to grow both flax and cotton and ship them both downriver.

"Well, you can do it," Elisha says, " but I ain't buying your property. I'll keep it for you, in case all your fancy plans go up. The money's just a loan."

"And what if they do go up?" Joseph asks. "You won't have nothing."

"It's our land, brother," Elisha says. "You always got a place to come home to."

Elisha knows, as the oldest child, he has a responsibility for the rest of the family, and there is no doubt he loves his brother. Besides, Elisha enjoys gambling and taking risks and this holds some charm for him.

"God damn it to all hell," he finally says. "If you're going to do it, you're going to do it. Let's go tell Pap and get it over with."

Elisha and Joseph had that conversation as they stood there looking both ways, Janus-like, at their property on either side of the gap, and at their past and their future. I know that as surely as I knew my brother and I were standing there, as if the earth were revealing each word with each step we took.

After several rests, my brother and I finally neared the end of our journey. Just above us was the flat where the meetinghouse once stood, and where Jack Damron once lived. Somewhere below us, lost in the trees and covered with generations of leaves, would be the flat where our father grew up, and where Jack and Farley played with him and protected him as long as they drew breath. Were trees still here, we wondered, where the dogs would have chased squirrels up into, or where Dad would have leaned against, resting from his own trips through these woods? Doubtful, I surmised. The Yellow Poplar Lumber Company of Ironton, Ohio clear-cut these hills in the 1890's; they would not have missed a salable tree, and no one knew how many times the resurgent growth had been sheared since then.

We came up on the flat and looked for the cemetery. We knew there were only five graves, but there had been no commercial headstones, even for Uncle Will, so we knew it might be difficult to find. The flat was easily big enough for a house seat, but as high as it was above the valley floor, it would probably have been difficult for a well to produce water during the fall season. Somehow, I sensed that this was where Elisha's son, George W, hid out during his frequent desertions from the Union Army. The first time or two a soldier deserted, he was usually just disciplined by the regiment. After that, he could easily have been shot or strung up. Although George's regiment, the 39th Kentucky, had the highest desertion rate in the Union Army, there was a limit to their patience. After his last absence, this time legitimately for measles, George stayed home and let the war end without him. I could sense he had stayed on that spot, listening at the window for riders approaching in the night, awaiting news of the War with the food his mother would bring him.

It was a peaceful place. The wind slipped gently through the trees and the sounds of traffic and commerce from the valleys below was muted. "I guess this is one of the reasons Lige liked to come up here," I told my brother. "He probably didn't like civilization all that much. Especially after Joseph died."

The flat sits on an elevated brow of Ripley Knob, its summit rising behind. I remembered the cemetery to be on a gap in the ridge between the flat and Ripley so we started down the hill toward the gap. Memories of Uncle Will's funeral and the difficult trek with his coffin to this place began to flood back. I had hoped I could rest beside his grave and shut my eyes and tune in to voices from the past, so that they could guide me in my work. I had so little with which to do so much. By last count there were nearly thirty unknown graves on the Prater and Samuel Robinson cemeteries. I had positively identified only a few; I knew I could not identify them all. I hoped something would possess me here, something that would infuse me with some special ability to see beyond the graves, so that I would not label as "Unknown" someone who once lived and breathed and loved and died in the arms of his family. I was hoping that hope when we found the cemetery. We found it, but we found even more.

On the Hopkins Creek side of the gap, loggers had systematically mowed down the trees in anticipation of the strip mining that was soon to follow. Our spirits fell when we saw the devastation, although most of Hopkins Creek had already been so reduced and we were prepared. But I was not prepared for what I saw next.

"Son of a bitch!" I swore. "Those God damned sons of bitches! Look what those sorry bastards have done!"

In oaths that would make my great-great-great grandfather proud of me, I cursed what I saw before me. A prospecting road had torn through the cemetery, destroying most of the cemetery. It was the work of the coal company that now owned Hopkins Creek and it led down to the ravaged valley where the coal mining operation's whistles could be heard in the distance. Or it was the work of loggers the coal company sold their trees to, but either culprit was equally despicable.

A bulldozer had mindlessly plunged through the tiny graveyard, pushing earth and Uncle Will's rusted metal funeral home marker over the hill in an obvious effort to find a coal seam. The destruction of that simple place was nearly complete. Only Elisha's grave, with its fieldstone marker, was still intact.

"Those greedy whores," I continued to rant. "Bastards!"

My brother was blushing. I was inflamed. My fury was made worse by the lack of anything tangible of the coal company around on which to vent my spleen.

"God damn them to hell!" I swore at the absentee criminals who had befouled this sweet, small place. Lige's spirit, if it still hovered nearby, was probably amused, but I was furious. This was another example of the horror the coal industry had inflicted on this land. It was typical. At least the state had an obligation to care for graves that had to be moved for public works, as in the road project down below. The same laws bound coal companies, but what was not reported did not have to be accounted for. I cursed the company, the coal industry, the logging industry, and everyone who lived in the coalfields and let the companies control their lives. Through swimming eyes, I damned them all.

After a while, having exhausted my repertoire of foul language, I sat down beside my brother who was cleaning the leaves off Elisha's grave.

"Are you finished?" he asked.

"Motherfuckers. . ." I grunted. I forced my breathing to return to normal, and my heart rate was following suit. The damage was done; there was nothing I could do.

Was this what families must have felt during the War and long afterward, I wondered, when bodies of their loved ones were dug up from family cemeteries and rolled out onto the roads, because in life that person had supported either the North or the South? There were many accounts of such viciousness in these hills. Forgiveness did not come easily after the War, and I could understand why. A grave, more than anything, should be a sanctuary. I knew then I could never forgive, or forget, what happened on this violated mountaintop.

But my brother and I learned what we could from what remained of the cemetery, and I received no further vision. Perhaps I had even frightened off Elisha's shade. Only his grave was still defined, and I sat down beside it. Paul had finished there and had already begun cleaning off what remained of the cemetery. I wiped my eyes and began to help him with our work.

My brother had raked off the leaves and had cleared the moss from the front of the stones, but only Lige's stone had discernible markings. I picked up a handful of moist dirt and rubbed across the marks. As the sun dried the thin layer of mud, the deeper lines stayed wet and became readable. We learned only that Elisha Hopkins (with the "N" on his gravestone reversed) had died in July of 1909. There might have been more beneath the ground had we pulled out the stones for a closer look, but I had no desire to do that, and I had expended all my energy cursing the coal industry. The rest of the cemetery was mere shuffled earth and pieces of rock. There was hollowness in one place that indicated, ominously, a coffin just under the surface. I suspected it was Will's, and I saw ghastly images of his arthritic bones crushed under bulldozer treads.

If there were spirits awaiting me, they would have scattered like mourning doves when I began my malediction. But since I merely echoed the language of my progenitor, there were probably few spirits there anyway, Lige having driven them away long ago.

I was tired now, much more tired than my brother and we worked only a few more minutes, taking some pictures and making notes. After a short rest, we began our return journey back down the mountain, pausing to revisit the ruins of the old mining operation or to allow me to curse again the new mining company just over the ridge. Covered with vegetation, the ruins of the old operation, with its many concrete pylons still upright, looked like a massive garden of stone, with markers for each of the men whose lives were taken by the mines.

How many of those men were the children, grandchildren, or great-grandchildren of Elisha? Elisha was born in 1815, in the same Virginia county as JEB Stuart, and Elisha's brother had been captured while defending the great Confederate salt works owned by Stuart's brother. By the time of his death in

1909, Elisha had seen a young nation come to adolescence, and another nation born and die, and now he rested on a lonely mountaintop where a modern age, with no respect for the past, attempted to obliterate any remembrance of him. Did he see this coming? Did he indeed have a second sight?

My brother and I retraced our route back down the hill, stumbling often in the retreating evening. The shadows were long by the time we returned to my Jeep and in its comfort, we dissected the success of our mission. Except for the date on Elisha's tombstone, carved by hand into a flat rock, we learned nothing new, but at least we had been children again. If my brother had not been the Public Health Director, and avidly anti-smoking, I would have brought along a cheap cigar to smoke as I did when I was young.

We drove out of Big Bug and around the base of the mountain. When we passed the little hollow where Uncle Will lived, I was thankful there had been gentle spirits like him in the world. *Why had he been like that, I wondered, when his father was the most irascible of men?* Perhaps, in his declining years, Elisha told Will about Joseph, and how this mountaintop was their world, and how the War brought that world to an end. Maybe he was more than the misanthrope everyone assumed he was. I hoped that was the case, and that Elisha was worthy of Uncle Will's love, and not merely a disgruntled, lonely, ridiculed old man at the end. Perhaps Uncle Will was the only one with whom he would share the glory of a distant Eden.

The evening had fallen and mists were swirling like lazy spirits awakened from sleep, trying to summon the will to rise up the mountainside and waft toward the top. I knew my father had watched these mists from his cabin with Jack and Farley lying beside him. I knew that Uncle Will had watched those same mists from his front porch, as well as Elisha and Joseph before him. But these formless clouds meandered, as they always had, in Empyrean ignorance of anyone watching them. It was as if they existed in another dimension, and only the shadow of that dimension was visible to us in this world.

Are there other dimensions, I wondered, somewhere in this limitless universe? And in one of them, could it be early summer as a young boy returns from school and begins to climb the upland trail to his home? Ahead, in the gathering dusk, is his mother and father, neither of which is truly his mother or father, although neither could love him any more if they were. The boy carries a fresh pie up the hill to his cabin, his dogs whining and jumping at him as he holds his prize high above his head, and he giggles at their impotence. The young mother who is smiling at her son is also hoping that there is some place in this world where he can be that happy forever.

In another dimension, or perhaps the same, are there two brothers who have walked from a place called Greasy Creek to a gap in the mountain where they can look at new land? It is a hot day, and honest sweat courses down their faces. Before them, there is new ground to break, to make into farmland and they rub their palms in anticipation of success. This is their place; they will be the first to claim it and it will bear their name. Here they will make their homes and the wilderness will be no more and their children and grandchildren and great-grandchildren and all their children will continue to work the land long after they are gone. And the two of them know that there is nothing in this world that can stop them for they are brothers and partners and together they are unstoppable.

If there is such a dimension, I conclude, then there is absolution after all; absolution for whatever sins have been committed in this one, for whatever debts that cannot be retired in this one. And love enough, at least enough, to overcome what inescapable heartbreak and cruelty abound in this life.

PART II

A Distant Eden

All the Geese Were Gone

"Do you want to go?" I asked my brother as we stood in Mom's kitchen, looking out the big windows, over the lawn that was once Harrison's garden. I had driven from Grassy Creek to Greasy Creek to give Paul the news I had just received that Caudill was dying. I was making plans to see him one last time.

"I don't think I can," Paul said. I understood. Since his father-in-law's death, his mother-in-law had sunk into much the same depression as our mother had since our father's death. Mom no longer lived at home, and was living in a retirement home now, doing well after years of regression. Paul and Vicky had to face the same problem with her mother, and it was a full-time job, staying with her at night and answering countless phone calls during the day.

"They know you're busy," I told him. "They'll understand if you can't come."

"How's John Paul taking it?" Paul asked me.

"Well, he's a doctor, so he's clinical about it," I told him. "He said Caudill's got about two months.

"But I don't think it's really hit him yet," I continued. "It probably won't, fully, until his dad's gone."

Across the lawn, a great rose bush that my mother had moved to the edge of the garden when my father made it into a lawn had grown nearly to the top of the tree she placed it near. Its pink roses appeared nearly white in the afternoon sun.

121

"Did I tell you what Mary Wright told me about that rose bush?" I asked my brother. I wanted to change the topic, to give my brother a chance to absorb another loss.

"No," he replied. "What'd she say?"

"She said Dorcus planted it, from her own rose bushes after Harrison moved up here. She said Harrison told her once that his mother and her grandmother were 'covering him up' with flowers."

"Who was Mary's grandmother?" Paul asked.

"Adelaide Sanders. Mom called her 'Aunt Adelaide.' She was Joe Phillips sister." Paul remembered the name; Joseph Phillips was Zachariah's son and our great-great grandfather who had died years before we were born.

"And that's the same bush?"

"Yeah, it's a good thing Mom moved it over there to save it. You know how Pop used to mow down every one of Mom's flowers."

We both laughed. My father was a hard worker, but not very precise in his efforts. Mom was constantly after him for obliterating the hollyhocks she attempted to grow near the edge of the yard.

"Tell John Paul we'll be thinking about him," my brother said, returning to the issue at hand. "It'll be hard for him since he was an only child. Is Hazel okay?"

"As far as I know," I said. "I just hope John Paul doesn't have the problems with his mother we had with ours."

Paul nodded his agreement. He regretted not going, but simply had too many responsibilities right now to make a trek to Ohio with me. Families were smaller now, and flung out all over the map. It was not like it was in previous generations, when families lived near each other and houses were awash in children.

When my brother left, I was still standing at the kitchen sink, looking out over the lawn at Dorcus' roses. Every time Caudill would visit, he would talk about the old days and the old house Pearl torched. With Rissie's home in the camps torn down and strangers living in Frank's house in Snake Branch, there was only this spot on Greasy Creek for the family to have some connection with the past.

And now no one lives here, I thought.

Caudill was the last of my boyhood heroes to die. The first was Avery, then my father and now the closest thing to a Hopkins uncle I had; all of them were gone like the houses they grew up in. They survived everything war had thrown at them; saw family and friends die on foreign soil and came home relatively intact. Marvin and Avery came back to the mines, and Caudill had gone north to escape them, but they had their memories of Greasy Creek to sustain them while they were serving their country. I thought about Caudill's slowly tarnishing Silver Star, the one he won in Korea fighting the Reds in the bitter cold north of Seoul, just as my father and Avery fought Nazis in the equally freezing German plains less than a decade before.

My grandfather also fought the Germans, but in a previous generation. I knew little about his war, although there were times he would reveal things to me, perhaps without knowing he had. When I was very young, he would bounce me on his knee and occasionally rasp out part of a song from his Army days:

Oh, we'll bake a cherry pie,
And we'll smash him in the eye,
And there won't be a Kaiser any more.

I didn't know the Kaiser, so I supposed he had been smashed in the eye, and it seemed to delight my grandfather as much as it did me. I suspect he sang that song while sitting in a small café with his fellow soldiers, stomping time on the floor as they sang. I often wonder if my father or my uncle had patronized the same café. It seemed hideously futile to have fought the same war twice, and then leave the next generation to fight their former allies.

But at that time there were clear reasons to fight. All three men left their homes to fight for America, to preserve the life they had, and to come back, if possible, to the place where they led it. Some, of course, would never see home again. On the Old Prater, Charlie Lewis and Ghomer Prater, boyhood chums of my father and Avery's cousins, rested under the ground they had helped clean countless times for Decoration Day. Their last sights on earth were not of Greasy Creek, but were of alien places in Europe or the Pacific, places whose names they could not even pronounce.

But what of that older age, long before the Great War, when Greasy Creek had no coal mines and the mountains were the same as they were ten thousand years before? What was it like to have lived then, before the Civil War came, before ruin settled across the peaceful coves that had never known war? How did the boys of Greasy Creek reconcile the fact that the conflict in front of them was not with an alien enemy, but with their own friends, and sometimes, with their own brothers or cousins? Since then, war had been relatively simple: the Japs were little yellow men, subhuman according to the propaganda, and the Krauts had fought us twice, so they deserved to be destroyed. But none of the boys of the Twentieth Century wars would have fought their brothers and their friends, like they did in the Nineteenth Century.

In 1860, as war clouds gathered on the Carolina coast, Greasy Creek was still part of only one country, and its people buried their dead for eternity, after wondrous, hard, beautiful lives of toil and accomplishment. Now, as the Old Prater lurched toward oblivion, it was incomprehensible to me that my family at one time had to choose sides.

In the five years since my father's death, I had learned more of the Civil War than I had in a lifetime of study. For most of my life, I ascribed the xenophobia and sullen ignorance of my race to the discarded genes of people I thought were not capable of enduring a further journey west. I thought my people dropped anchor in the mountains simply because it was easier than going on.

I did not give my ancestors credit, for I assumed every stereotype I ever heard of mountaineers had a nugget of truth in it. My family was an exception, of course, for you are allowed to make myths of the people you love. But I thought my father and the men and women of my family were in opposition to the DNA that was given them. But I thought the Old Ones, as Rissie called them, were just hermits, with no interest in the affairs of the day, of the world outside their deep valleys.

I know now they were no hermits.

I know now that before the War, before the timber barons, before the coal barons, and before the Great Society and the Appalachian Regional Commission, that geography was not a major hindrance to the commerce, intellectual and otherwise, of the time. I greatly erred by assuming otherwise. The stereotypes came later, after the War and after the uneasy peace of ensuing generations.

I have aggrieved the spirits of my ancestors by comparing them to their descendants. I have attributed too much of the baseness of life in these hills today to a legacy not wrought by my ancestors. I assumed that the fatalism so common, and the diminution of spirit so pervasive in my culture, existed before the mines came, that it was indigenous to my breed.

But I was so wrong.

My comparison was not valid, could not be valid. Where members of a crippled race now shuffle purposelessly through their lives, at one time giants walked here. To compare their descendants to them would be false and unfair, like comparing apples to oranges, or titmice to eagles.

Mary Wright helped disabuse me of my prejudice. We talked often about Zachariah Phillips, from whom she and I both descended, and she told me about his death.

"He got back from the war," she said, "and the children were starving. He went down to Winright's house and tried to buy some corn to grind. He wouldn't sell him any and Zach tried to take some anyway. The children were starving. That old man killed him right there as he was trying to climb the stairs into the loft."

"Where was this?" I asked.

"Down on Gillespie Fork. Where Tommy Adkins' house is now."

Mary then said something that awakened me as if I had been pulled from slumber, not like a bell in the night, but more like a deep silence in the house that awakens the sleeping with its gravity: "Winright's old place stood there for years and years. They just tore it down not too long ago."

My ears perked up at that remark.

"How long ago?" I asked. The older one gets, the shorter the years become, and I wondered what "not too long ago" meant to Mary.

"It was not long after the boys came back from the war. World War II."

"Could it have been in the early Fifties?" I asked.

"Yeah," she said. "I guess it was. It was just an old log cabin that had been added on to."

"Did it have a window to the right of the front door."

She thought for a minute and said: "It did, now that I remember."

"And a narrow set of stairs to the left as you came in the door?" I asked.

"It sure did. Do you remember it?"

"I think so," I said. "There was a stain on the floor at the bottom of the stairs. Was it a bloodstain?"

"Yeah," she said. "They never could get it up. It stayed there until they tore down the old house."

It was a spring day when my parents put me in the seat between them in my father's Packard, and we drove down the hollow to where an old house was being demolished. There was debris in the yard as we approached the front door of an ancient log cabin that appeared the middle of what used to be a frame house. Peeling white siding was stacked in piles around the yard, and the remnants of a stone chimney to the right of the cabin was crumbling to the ground. There was no roof.

My parents clutched my hands tightly as we walked to the cabin, for fear I would run mindlessly into the rusty nails that stuck out from the broken siding.

Inside the door, the sunlight slipped through the cracks of the ceiling and illuminated layers of old linoleum that had been peeled back from the floor to reveal an ugly brownish-black splotch on the rough wood beneath. My father spoke to one of the workmen and he paused to extend an arm toward the spot. My mother raised her right hand to her chin and spoke to the man as well. After a while, we left. Once or twice during the following weeks, the topic would be raised again in family conversations, in hushed tones, and from what I could pick up, the spot was the bloodstain of someone in my family who had died there. I forgot about it until Mary unlocked the memory nearly fifty years later.

There were other such incidents. Someone would say something to me, and some rusty machinery in my brain would begin to grind, like tumblers in an old combination lock falling into place. I would recall some event of the past where a part of my family history was revealed to me and I was either too young or too reckless to care about its significance. Even as a child, I knew these things were somehow taboo; that the family would not speak of them too openly and I remembered that furtiveness more than I remembered the actual details.

Indeed, the reason why I thought I knew much less was that some things were just not talked about. A hundred years after the Civil War, people on Greasy Creek were still cautious, still afraid of possible repercussions from talking too freely about what their families did during the War. This reticence was pervasive throughout the mountains. It is one of the most enduring legacies of the War and few of my generation know it even exists or how subconsciously it colors our acts and deeds.

Until recently, there were no monuments to soldiers of the Civil War in eastern Kentucky, aside from the weathered regimental tombstones that marked their graves. In neighboring Floyd County, the past has been paid more homage with a new monument erected to the Battle of Ivy Mountain and a new National Historic Battlefield designation given to the Battle of Middle Creek.

Virginia and Tennessee, Southern states to our east and south, have their stone Confederate soldiers in front of nearly every courthouse. The illusion is, of course, that those states were unified during the War, and unified in their mourning for the Confederate cause, but both states, and in fact every Southern state except for South Carolina, furnished regiments to the North as well as the South. But Virginia, having bled more than any other Southern state, may be allowed some discretion in its selective memory.

West Virginia, as close to Greasy Creek as Virginia, was the only state to actually gain something from the War, and has an occasional monument to its sons, but in Eastern Kentucky, which sent many more men into battle, such memory has been deafeningly silent. Other parts of Kentucky have their statues and cenotaphs; but in the hills, except for the soldier's tombstones, there was nearly nothing until a few historians began discovering the awesome story of the Civil War in these hills. Monuments and roadside markers are finally appearing, a hundred years after they should have been erected, but at least something has been done to remind the current generation of the sacrifices of a much older one.

Some 80,000 Kentucky boys fought for the North; just less than half that number fought for the South. My great-great-great grandfathers, their sons, their brothers, and their friends were on both sides of the conflict, and some even changed sides during it. But by the end of the War, it was almost as if they wanted to forget it ever happened. But it did happen, and although they tried, it could never be put aside.

In 1890, the federal government commissioned a Special Census of surviving Union veterans of the Civil War to determine both the number still living and what their needs were. The regular 1890 National Census was almost entirely destroyed in a fire, and the Special Veteran's Census is practically all genealogists have left, but it is even more valuable because of the essential error the census takers made. It listed Confederate soldiers as well as Union soldiers, as if the enumerators felt the Rebs deserved some acknowledgment as well, or perhaps, forty years later, the Eastern Kentuckians on the census might have forgotten whose flag they served.

There were more Union than Confederate soldiers on the Special Census in Pike County, since more Union soldiers served. But almost uniformly, their conditions are worse. I suspect that merely indicates the Union soldiers had more to eat and were better cared for during the war, improving their chances of longevity. And although many former Confederates joined the Union Army before the War ended and did not mention their Confederate service, there were simply fewer Rebs still living in 1890.

Among the survivors of either side, the most common complaint was hemorrhoids and rupture. Hemorrhoids resulted from riding for long periods of time without answering the call of nature, and no sphincter muscle was ever relaxed when the soldier knew there was death awaiting him around any bend in the road.

Being thrown against the pommel of a saddle by a gun-shy horse permanently separated the abdominal muscles of many a cavalryman; and the morning routine of coughing up the dust of the previous day's ride and the soot of strong tobacco compounded the damage.

These were not glorious wounds, but they were painful and sometimes fatal. Medicine had advanced greatly since the Civil War, and in many ways because of it, but there was yet little treatment for these maladies in 1890. The men who had served on horseback through the miserably hot, humid summers of the mountains and their equally miserable bone-chilling winters, with poor food and little time for personal hygiene, were reminded constantly of that service with bloody pants and painful trusses.

Since most of the troops were farmers before the war, that was the occupation they returned to, and it is not difficult to imagine what it was like for them to clear land and break new ground with their intestines bulging against the thin veneer of their skin.

Working the land and raising stock was the major occupation for Pike Countians at the end of the Nineteenth Century as it was in the beginning. But the experiment in cotton farming, which Joseph Hopkins was so successful at, was never repeated. Some cotton was still raised, and my family still has Clarinda Phillips' cotton cards, but no one ever attempted to grow it commercially again. In fact, farming itself changed dramatically after the War. The rich bottomland, close by the rivers and creeks, where crops were raised in abundance for the families who farmed it, was neglected in the last years of the War. What good was it to sweat and toil when it would just be stolen or eaten up when foragers came through?

Families turned to plots higher up in the mountains where the soil was poorer, but the location ensured some security. After the War, families still retained their "top gardens." As the family farms were broken up into smaller farms for succeeding generations and increasing numbers of mouths to feed required more farmland, those isolated places continued to be farmed. That is, until the mines made farming in Pike County an anachronism.

Most Civil War soldiers from Pike County survived the fighting, but the world they left did not. Their families had nearly given up on farming the bottomlands, and the fields were covered with weeds and brush. The split-rail fences that neatly divided good neighbors were gone, burned as fuel in soldier's campfires. When attempts were made at re-establishing the old boundaries, there was always resistance, and it was not unusual to see boundary disputes end in violence.

Farming became less diversified after the War, as cultivation of crops like flax and millet waned in favor of corn. That ancient weed could feed both the mountain soldier's family and his farm animals, and although corn often repulsed him because he had eaten so much of it while in service, he learned to accept it because he had no other choice. The diversity of farm animals shrunk as well, with families concentrating on hogs and cattle for market, although no homestead would be without its chicken coop.

The hogs that survived the war did so because their owners cut unique marks on their ears and released them to feed on the mast of acorns and buckeyes that covered the hillsides. If hogs were kept in pens during the war, foragers stole them, or they were the victims of other families whose own stock had been stolen. Disputes often arose as to who these wild hogs actually belonged to, and one famous hog trial contributed to the most famous feud in the United States when the Hatfield and McCoy clans each claimed the same animal.

Chicken coops and corncribs fell into disrepair during the War because no one was there to maintain them, and they would not have been used anyway. Food was desperately protected and both animals and grain were brought inside the cabins themselves. Food that could be picked and dried was kept in the lofts so it could be protected at gunpoint, and often was.

Sheep and goats became rare, as they were easily stolen and expensive to replace for the quantity of meat they supplied when compared to beef. Geese, which once furnished families with eggs and meat, disappeared from mountain cognizance, an even greater loss in comfort and security. While goose eggs were much richer than chicken eggs, and a fine goose for dinner was once a desirable treat for the English-descended mountaineer, food was not the greatest benefit obtained from raising geese. The down for fine featherbeds, which the geese supplied, also disappeared, and many families, in their poverty, were lucky to have a feather bed with chicken feathers and often made beds with corn shucks as padding, if they were lucky enough to have a bed frame. But even that loss was not the greatest.

Geese were the best security system the mountaineer could have and protected his home with a ferocity unmatched by even the most loyal cur. Indeed, it was rare to see a dog battle a charging, hissing goose, as the latter was almost always the winner in such contests. Geese were the resplendent emperors of their domains, and they strolled about their farms with a regal detachment, fearing nothing. Practically none survived the War, ending up over a campfire at the end of a soldier's bayonet or as the last meal for a starving family in a cast iron kettle with whatever would pass for dumplings. The very few that survived saw the extinction of their race by gangs of wild dogs that ran unfettered through the hills, their former owners unconcerned, or dead themselves.

The sheep and the goats and the geese were gone, as was an entire way of life, and the soldier returned to a place where he had to start over again, to rebuild what had once been a veritable Eden in the valleys and coves of Eastern Kentucky. Because of suspicion and fear, the mountain soldier's children never experienced the simple pleasures of their father's youth.

The children of Joseph Hopkins would never work the cotton fields again; by the end of the war, the land that had produced over a hundred 480-pound bales of cotton in 1860 were reduced to wasteland from neglect and trespass. In 1867, Henry May, a former comrade and from whom Joseph had purchased some of the 450 acres he farmed, bought the mortgage on the farm and foreclosed on Lucinda and her children. When the commissioner's deed for 100 acres of Joseph's best farmland was executed, Lucinda received $58.50. Joseph had purchased the property for $117.00 in 1857 and had paid one-half of the mortgage by 1862 when the war closed the New Orleans cotton market. She stayed there for another decade, selling off in parcels what was once the most prosperous farm in Pike County in order to survive. When the last of her children was safely married, she sold the home she had shared with Joseph and moved back to Greasy Creek to live with her daughter until she died.

Like most hard-core Confederates in Pike County, Henry was himself the object of several lawsuits after the war, most notably by Col. John Dils, Jr., who formed the 39th Kentucky Mounted Infantry USA, the 10th Kentucky's arch enemy.

Abraham Lincoln dismissed Dils from his post for personal and professional misbehavior and he never received the redress he sought for what he considered a political attack on his character. The many lawsuits he filed against former Confederates, including the one against Henry, was a means of demonstrating the very real losses his fortune and his reputation had suffered. Henry had little choice but to use whatever means he had to pay off his liabilities, hence his action against the widow and children of his former comrade. It did little good; Henry left Pike County penniless, broken in fortune and spirit.

Henry's cabin stood for many years in Pike County, and, like so many other Civil War cabins, was eventually expanded into a larger house. It was demolished to make way for a petroleum tank farm in the 1980's. Before then, my great-uncle Jerome Brown wrote his memoirs in that house. Those were the same stories my great-aunt burned after his death.

By 1870, civil government was restored in Pike County and schools were functioning again, but there was never again the trust in government or government officials that had once existed when men felt confident their voices could be heard. Courts became bogged down in the sheer volume of lawsuits filed against former Confederates to recover losses from the War. A substantial amount of property changed hands, the result of both legitimate debts and the hand of politicians who knew then, as they do now, how to pick juries. Many pioneers who had carved homes and new lives from the wilderness now slept under the soil their children no longer owned.

Few people trusted anyone after the War; there was too much loss and too many memories of betrayal and hard times. Until the timber barons came to Pike County in the late 1800's, presaging its final plundering by the coal barons after the turn of the century, an uneasy peace settled over the hollows. There was some reconciliation as the children and grandchildren of Civil War soldiers began to marry the offspring of their former enemies, but it was not until timber and coal created new jobs for the mountaineers that the animosities of the past truly began to fade.

My great-great-great grandfather William David Coleman served with the 39th during the War. An easygoing, generous man, whom everyone called "Dave," he had homes both on Greasy Creek on the Levisa Fork of the Big Sandy River and also on Peter Creek, fifty miles away, on the Tug Fork of that same watershed. At first it was simple wanderlust that caused him to move from place to place. The grass is always greener somewhere else, he would think. He volunteered for combat at age 37. He had a large enough family to keep the farm going during his absence, and perhaps he thought it would be fun. But when he came back from the War, his smile had disappeared, and he moved back and forth even more. Eternally restless, he seemed to be always looking over his shoulder, and once left Greasy Creek for Peter Creek without harvesting the corn crop he had worked so hard growing during the summer.

When he died he was buried, as was his wish, at the head of one of the most isolated hollows on Greasy Creek. It was as if he sought his final rest in a place so remote no one would venture there to desecrate his grave and no demons from his past would haunt his shade.

Gail Mays once told me she could never figure out why our ancestor moved back and forth so much, leaving family in both locations. Until I talked to Gail, I did not know I even had kinfolk on Peter Creek, and I never knew any of the Colemans there. In fact, I never knew much of my Coleman family at all. Neither did my father, whose mother had died when he was still nursing. Dad's grandfather, Paris Coleman, moved away from Greasy Creek to Oak Hill, Ohio, after the family shoot-out in 1926. They never came back to live, although I still have vague memories of a big, white-haired old man who would stay with us occasionally. I remember only his looking at me with sadness, and I know now it was his longing for the daughter who died before she saw her son grow out of infancy, let alone see the grandson who stared questioningly back at her father.

Paris had already buried his wife Nina in Ohio when he came back to visit. She was the daughter of another soldier of the 39th, Robert Damron. Her brother John A. Damron,

Robert's only other child to live into adulthood, married Paris' sister Nona. Robert was 21 when the war began and was my great-great grandfather. Where most of my Civil War ancestors were great-great-great, Robert qualified for one less great, having married later than most of his fellow soldiers.

Robert founded what became the Greasy Creek Old Regular Baptist Church and preached forgiveness to a congregation always uneasy from the War. Robert soon moved to Little Creek, just over the hill from Greasy Creek, but he continued his ministry on Greasy Creek until his death. When he died, he was buried on a point overlooking what was once Joseph Hopkins' farm. While he was alive, he would ride his horse through the gap between the two creeks to the Greasy Creek Regular Baptist Church which met then, as its descendant, the Greasy Creek Old Regular Baptist Church, still does, for two days every month, according to the old circuit rider schedule. Robert Damron outlived his friend and fellow soldier Dave Coleman by many years, and he passed the hollow where Dave was buried every time he made the trip. I often wonder what this kindly preacher thought as he passed his friend's burial ground, and if he mouthed a silent prayer for Dave's soul as well as his own.

When Ezekiel Prater moved to Greasy Creek and bought the land on which the Old Prater now rested, there were already Hopkins buried there. Cornelius and Dorcus were buried just up on the hill from the cabin their children had built for them, and it was a simple decision to bury the Prater dead there as well.

Zeke was another mountain patriarch with many children, although he had begun his family in Floyd County. His first wife was Mary Reffit, known as Polly in the vernacular of the day, and after the War, he left her to move in with Rhoda Sanders, who left her husband to be with Zeke. By 1870, he set up housekeeping with her, but he also moved Polly and the children next to him. But by 1880, Rhoda was gone, and he married Polly again, returning a certain social legitimacy to his children. And unlike Elisha, he was content with only two wives in his life. He lived until 1910, and Daniel Jackson Prater, his son and my great-great grandfather, outlived him by only four years.

Daniel Jack is buried on the Old Prater at the head of Zeke's grave, along with his wife, Melissa, who is buried beside him. Granny Melissy, as everyone called her, died in 1953, not long after my seventh birthday. I remember looking into her coffin and seeing her gnarled hands at rest across her body. Earlier that spring, she hid Easter eggs for us at my grandmother Lexie's house while my mother distracted us, and those tiny hands were too arthritic to completely conceal them. When we were released to the search, I started to fill up my basket without shame until I realized my selfishness. I reconsidered and helped my brother find his share and then helped my mother find the rest of them for my sister who was, of course, too young to have the slightest idea of what we were doing.

I had forgotten all about it until the memory flooded back one Easter as I sat on the cemetery near Ezekiel's grave and recalled my great-great grandmother, and how lucky I was to have known her.

Melissy's father, James Roberts, Jr., was in the 10th with Joseph, and faced Zeke at Saltville. If either of these great-great-great grandfathers had killed the other, I would never have been born. But these two former enemies each gave one of their children to the other and the Prater clan on Greasy Creek evolved from them. Such marriages were not uncommon as the century waned, and the Civil War was without a champion in Daniel Jack and Melissy's house.

Henry D Adkins, another comrade from the 39th, is buried at the foot of Zeke's grave. Not long before his death, he married one of Zeke's granddaughters. But it was only a marriage of convenience, a way that Henry could have someone take care of him since his wife, Bethina, had divorced him long ago, hating him for his work at Saltville. She was Dorcus' older sister, and like Dorcus, she had no qualms about taking sides, even though their father could not. Elisha's daughters were stubborn and could never forgive the loss of their Uncle Joe. Dorcus, at least, carried that bitterness to her own grave.

Aside from Melissy, none of my Confederate family was buried on the Old Prater, although I suspect if such things happen, Zach and Joseph's ghosts would have wound their way through its moss-covered stones, swapping phantasmal tobacco and sharing stories with their former enemies.

Zachariah did not die during the War, but the War killed him as surely as it killed Joseph in that meadow outside Bloomfield.

In the Battle of Saltville, Joseph was captured and marched back to Lexington to his eventual doom, although Zachariah did not know his fate until the battle was over. Only later did he learn of Joe's loss, and wished he could have been taken in his stead.

After the last threadbare troops were called out of Southwest Virginia by Lee to help the Army of Northern Virginia fight its last battle against Grant, Zachariah still held on to his beliefs. He fought all the way to the Confederacy's last moments and was arrested, along with the other final guards of Jefferson Davis, when the President was captured in Irwinville, Georgia, on May 11, 1865.

After his parole, Zachariah came back to Greasy Creek to patch back together whatever he could from his former life. He knew that what he left would not be there when he returned. He knew his wife had been reduced to prostitution to keep their family alive, and she had borne a child who was not his, and he had known this long before he began his final battle. Yet he still fought on.

In the last weeks of the War, Zachariah stayed with his colonel when the call came from Lee. Petersburg had fallen and Richmond was abandoned. Every available soldier was needed in the east. Lee was moving away from Richmond to find ground of his choosing to meet Grant. When they heard the news, the boys who had lost so much in the backwater of Southwest Virginia were ready to regain their honor, regardless of the cost, including death. Perhaps they even preferred death. But it was not to be, at least right away, for Zachariah.

When the 10th got to Christiansburg, about halfway across the state, it found the remnants of Lee's army straggling back from Appomattox. Basil Duke, John Hunt Morgan's brother-in-law and the last commander of the Southwest Virginia Brigade released his men to go home if they wished, although he would head south. Only one-tenth of the 650 men remaining chose to go home. Zach stayed with Duke as they turned for North Carolina where Joe Johnston was still in the field against Sherman.

They might have made it, only in time to have that army surrender as well, but near the state line they intercepted the Confederate government fleeing Danville, Virginia where it had last convened. The 10th Kentucky Cavalry, mountain boys who had no illusions about their fate and the fate of the rest of the South, gladly joined the final guard of Jefferson Davis and protected him until his capture.

Family history says Zach had walked home from Georgia when he arrived back on Greasy Creek in late summer of 1865, but I discounted the story. Our boys would never have been given such a chance for glory, I thought, but again I was wrong.

My mother told me that when she was a child, her mother would dispatch her to stay with Aunt Adelaide Sanders, Zachariah's last child, and then a widow in her seventies. Adelaide was a tiny, bent woman who would sometime startle guests at her house with her habit of standing up suddenly, breaking wind loudly, and sitting back down to resume her conversation as if nothing had happened. Among the stories Adelaide would tell would be the story of how "Daddy was with Jeff Davis at the end."

When Jefferson Davis rejoined the Confederate government wagon train in its flight, he intended a dash for the Trans-Mississippi and held out hope for a last redoubt in Texas. With the Kentucky boys around him, he dismissed the rest of the tattered regiments and headed into Georgia with the

Kentuckians as his final guard. Selecting ten volunteers to accompany him, he began the trek only to have it interrupted in Irwinville with his arrest. Zachariah Phillips, who had given nearly everything he had to the Cause, was also arrested and with his parole, headed back to the mountains where little of what he once knew now awaited him.

In spite of being privileged to watch the final act of this country's greatest tragedy, there was no glory for him when he came home. Clarinda, deluged with guilt and shame, had given up her enterprise and was waiting for him when he came up the dusty road that ran by their house. I suspect she did not know if he could even look at her again, let alone be her husband.

Another scene formed in my mind as I stared through the window at the rose bush climbing toward heaven. Did this really happen, I wondered? Or am I just romanticizing what I do not know? But what could be romantic about the awful scene unfolding in front of me?

There was a garden, but it had been planted late, and would yield little. Not enough to sustain them this winter; not even enough to sustain them the rest of the warm days of late summer. There was no money. Her customers had been sent away at the point of a gun, and her cheeks were sunken with dark circles under her eyes, from the starvation and the tears that flowed constantly. Her skin, like the skin of her children, is sallow, and like her children, she has lost teeth. But she has little reason to smile.

The children barely recognize their father as he limps toward them. He has no horse, and has walked all the way from Georgia with Mexican money in his pocket, since there were no horses to buy in that ruined country.

There had been too many faces of men at the cabin in the past two years, and their father's face was not the smiling red-bearded face they once remembered. Joseph, the youngest boy, named for the Uncle Joe Hopkins that has been a year now in his grave, runs sobbing into his father's arms. Clarinda stands in the little garden, twisting her hands until he comes to her.

139

What did he say to her that day, or she to him? The house where they lived is long gone, but there is an eerie resonance from the ground when I visit the site, as if the moment of his return was just that day, as if the air still crinkles with the charged ions of that inexpressible scene. The house site can be seen from the the lower cemetery, where three of their infant children lay. Two were born dead in 1857 and I find no markers for their graves. However, another who died in 1851 has a tombstone, but it does not mark his grave and was apparently flung there as the grave was obliterated. On that stone are carved only three initials: FMP. Zachariah named his son for Francis Marion, the Swamp Fox, the Revolutionary War hero he hoped to emulate in what was for him a second war of American liberation.

At one time I suspected Zach's lost patriotism was the real reason for his death. With nothing left to live for, his recklessness was just another suicide mission, like the one he was assigned when the 150 boys of the 10th Kentucky tried to stop 5200 Union soldiers marching toward Saltville. Who could ever know why he forced the hand of his wife's cousin when he demanded food that no one had to give him? His children were starving, but who would feed them if he were dead?

I was told he died in October, the same month that George Hopkins married his first cousin Victoria, and possibly the same month that she died. Was his rage uncontrollable, or did he wish an end to the torment of living day by day in a world that had unalterably changed? I could see that rage, however, as if something narrated the tale for me and I had no doubt it happened just as I was told.

"Hallo, the cabin," he yells. "Winright, are you there? I need some corn for my children. I got money."

"I ain't got nothin' for you, Zach," Winright replies. " I ain't got enough for my own." He opens the door slightly, to make the announcement official, but soon slams it back and slides the wooden bolt home.

"Well, God damn you. You give me another mouth to feed and, by God, you're going to help me feed it."

With the fury of years of bitter combat behind him, he smashes the door open into Winright's cocked pistol. Neither man has any illusions; their bond, forged in the crucible of war had dissolved the instant the cabin door burst open. Their eyes lock as Zachariah begins his final charge. It is not for country or for a lost idea of freedom; it is simply for food, for the lives of his children, and perhaps, a dismissal of Winright as an enemy, a way of smashing back at the man for the pain Clarinda had caused him.

Neither man has any choice, and Winright shoots him at the foot of the rude stairway leading up to the loft of the cabin.

Zachariah staggers forward and falls on his face, his blood and his life pouring out on the puncheon floor.

How do I know this stark vision is true? What makes me relive that hateful scene every time I pass the place where Winright's cabin once stood?

Then a voice asks me: why do you wonder? You saw his blood yourself.

It remained on Winright's floor for ninety years.

Clarinda buried her husband and never married again. When she died in 1904, my great-great grandfather Joseph buried her beside his father, who forgave her before he died. I suspect Joseph did also, but I wonder if their older boy, John, ever forgave his mother for her sins, or his father for leaving them. After Zachariah's death, he went as far away from Kentucky as he could and settled in Washington State. I often envy him for leaving; I was unsuccessful each time I tried.

There are no photographs of Zachariah; indeed, I have not one picture of the men I have written about, but in my mind there is a physiognomy for each them. I have drawn it in my mind from the features of their descendants, and I see them in my mirror every morning.

There is a picture of Clarinda, taken perhaps twenty years after Zachariah's death and it reveals the horror of what had happened to her. Her hair is still dark, as are her features, but the weight of all that had gone before has pulled down the skin around her eyes and mouth. Her hands are rough and coarse as they rest in her lap, but they are the hands of a thousand mountain women who cooked meals and rang dinner bells and washed clothes with the harsh lye soap of the era. There is no clue to whose faces those hands once caressed, but her face, never again to feel the touch of her husband's hands, is a tableau of misery.

If a face could reflect the loss of a husband, hers does, but the horror that etched those lines and that wide-eyed stare had other geneses. Not only had she lost Zachariah, she had lost three of her four brothers in Confederate service. Only her brother Winright, cousin to the man of the same name who killed her husband, came back. Her brothers Moses, John Henry, and Eli did not, although rumors would pass about one of the Adkins boys who did not really die, but left for the West for a new life where there would be no grudges and no killing.

Dave Coleman gave her a farm to sustain her through the rest of her life after Zachariah's death. He also gave her another child. I wonder if she turned to him because no one else would be kind to her. She is buried on that farm, next to Zachariah, whom she placed there forty years before she died. After Dave, she had no other lovers.

She does not look directly at the camera in this picture; it is as if she has allowed it to be taken only for her children's sake, and on her face there is still the unmistakable expression of disbelief, of utterly incomprehensible loss. Or perhaps it is merely the result of seeing so many eyes turn away from her, and she no longer finds it necessary to search the face of those to whom she speaks. Whatever the case, I suspect she wore that face in her coffin.

There is another picture of the Phillips family I treasure. It is an old photograph of me in my mother's arms, taken in front of the two-room house my father built after he came back from World War II. It is September 1946 and it is the first picture of me after my birth and Rissie took it with the camera she

142

purchased years before with the wages Harlan worked out in the Greasy Creek mine.

Beside my mother stands my grandmother Lexie Hamlin Prater, and beside her is my great-grandmother Effie Phillips Hamlin. Beside her is my great-great grandmother Rosa Courtney Phillips, wife of Joseph Phillips. Five generations are standing there, although I, wrapped in a blanket Rosa gave me, am not really standing. I try to decipher the picture, to see if there is anything I can glean from their expressions; to see if there is something there that can tell me what it was like to have a part of one's family lost so ignobly, but there is nothing. The picture, like the graves where Zachariah and Clarinda sleep, is silent.

Behind us is the shadow, in black-and-white, of Dorcus' pale pink roses.

I still have the camera; it is the only tangible thing I have left of my grandmother, and I often wonder what images were recorded by its lens. What Hopkins or Praters or Colemans or Phillips once stood before my grandmother to have their pictures taken for some special occasion? Funerals were popular times for picture-making on Greasy Creek, when families united again, if only in grief. How many grief-stricken visages were captured on silver halide and made indelible, at least for a while? Were there photographs of women in her lost collection, women who waited patiently for their husbands to return from the mines, or men whose lives were snuffed out inside the mountains Elisha Hopkins once owned?

Elisha did not serve in the War, but two of his brothers and one of his sons did. He was too old to serve, if an excuse was warranted, but I often wondered if he rode with any of the gangs that exacted retribution for trespasses from former friends or relatives. I do not believe he did, and nothing was told to me to contradict that belief. I know it had nothing to do with cowardice or bravery. He was, like so many men who stayed home, simply torn between his emotions for his brothers. When the War ended, Joseph was in his grave, and Columbus Christopher came back, as did all the boys in blue or gray, to no hero's welcome. Mercifully, "Lum" was in hospital during the Battle of Saltville, deathly ill, and did participate in the battle that saw his brother captured. When he came back, Elisha gave him the house he once shared with Mahala to raise his family. His children may not have been able to forgive their husbands or their Uncle Lum, but Elisha could not disown his brother.

In October of 1865, George married his first cousin Victoria, Joseph's oldest child, whom he had courted since they were children. By 1870, George was a widower, living with his mother again in Pike County and a five-year-old child named Rebecca Victoria. She was the only child George and Victoria would ever have, and I suspect she was born just before or very soon after her parents were married. Victoria may have died in childbirth, but I suspect she died of the measles George brought back from service. I also suspect he never forgave himself for what he did.

In 1883, Rebecca Victoria married a boy of her grandmother's line, but by the time the KYDOT threatened what remained of the lower cemetery, no one remembered where her mother had been laid.

I do not know where she is buried, but I know it is one of the lost graves on that tiny, abused cemetery; somewhere, I suspect, near her brother John Miles. Long after her death, George married a niece of Ezekiel Prater, and moved to Prater Creek in Floyd County to live near her family. I could find no children of their marriage. I suspect the measles that took Victoria's life also robbed him of the ability to sire any more children.

Melissa knew all the graves on both cemeteries and kept Victoria's grave decorated as long as she lived. She loved the raven-haired little girl George brought back to visit. She even named her youngest daughter for Victoria or her daughter, or maybe them both. I found George's grave in another Prater Cemetery in Floyd County. After Rissie died, there was no one left on earth to remember Victoria's.

By 1870, Haley Blackburn, perhaps having enough of living as the third wife, left Elisha to return to her family on Johns Creek, about thirty miles from Greasy Creek. He tried to follow her. Her family, except for her younger brother Wilburn, known as "Monkey Will," did not want her back. Monkey Will served in three Confederate regiments during the War, but with his last capture, and under duress, became a "galvanized Yankee" and joined the 39th.

Another happy wastrel, Monkey Will cared little for what anybody thought; he was another mountaineer who lived life to the fullest, and even though he received a pension from the federal government, he named his grandson "Cero" after his favorite Confederate general. But as he had to bow to the overwhelming force of the Union Army, he had to bow to another force, just as powerful. Society began to reconstitute itself after the War, and among its first resumptions were prejudice and narrow-mindedness.

Haley's family shunned her for leaving her husband and two children for Elisha, by whom she had even more children. Even Monkey Will, with his engaging good humor so similar to Elisha's, could not combat the superciliousness of his own family. The last official record I found of Haley was when she stood up for her nephew, Allen Maynard, who loved his aunt in spite of his family, at a wedding in 1872.

In 1873, Elisha secured a land grant for 50 acres on Grassy Fork of Raccoon Creek, halfway between his family on Greasy Creek and Mahala's family on Johns Creek. Like a newlywed, he built a cabin and a barn there for the two of them, and plowed ground for their crops. But within a year she died. Elisha, whose heart was broken by Joseph's death, felt it crumble into dust. He called in the preachers for a wake, and asked her family to attend, but only Monkey Will and Allen came. My ghost spat venomously as he told me that story:

"Lige, I got to talk to you," Will said. "Those God damn women don't want me to bury Haley with the rest of the family."

For the first time, Elisha's power of expression failed him. The voice that could flay skin was choked back. In any other situation, he would have unleashed great blasphemous oaths that could set fire to the mountains with their vituperation, but now he was unable to summon even a small curse. He looked into Monkey Will's eyes for a moment, and then looked back at the cabin where Mahala's body lay in oblivion on the rope bed they shared when she was alive.

"Then I'll bury her here," he said.

"You know that's not what she wanted. She wanted to come home, Lige."

"Well, hell, they don't want her. Even now she's dead. God damn them. God damn them all."

"Listen here, Lige. The cemetery's on my property. Ain't no God damn woman going to tell me what I can do with my own property, and by God, there's a point just across from the cemetery where we'll put her. We used to play there when we was little, me and Haley. I know she'd like it."

He knew Will was right, and Elisha, who would never have been forced into making choices not of his own design, accepted the alternative Will offered him.

By themselves, Elisha, Monkey Will and Allen dug Haley's grave, and placed her in it, in the coffin Elisha had made for her. Elisha returned to the loneliness of the cabin on Grassy Fork he shared with her and for another winter and summer he lay drunk and rarely came out. Phoebe sued him for abandonment in 1877, which woke him up from his long alcoholic slumber. In 1878, he married again, for the last time, and moved back in with Phoebe with his new bride. After a while, having enough of life on the valley floor, he moved to the cabin he and his brother built on the mountain, on the gap between Greasy Creek and Hopkins Creek. He named one of his three boys for Monkey Will; that was the old man I helped bury in 1959, the old man who loved me because I looked like my father when he was a boy.

In the 1880 census, Elisha listed Phoebe as his widowed sister. The census taker knew no better, and it may have been the last practical joke he played on anyone. Even with a young wife, or perhaps because of it, he brooded for the rest of his life. His legacy, like most men's, was based on his final years, and those years were desolate. He was no longer just "Lige." He became "Ol' Lige," the scourge of Greasy Creek, the embodiment of bitterness. And he expended his rage and sorrows on anything or anyone near him, even anyone who tried to love him, and that word was lost from his vocabulary.

A hundred years later, Charlene and I bought our first house, and we moved into a giant four-story structure started by a local building contractor who went broke and died before finishing it. It was situated at the confluence of two small creeks, much like my father's house on Greasy Creek, and I could hear the stream burble as I went to sleep at night. In 1994, because I had far more room for a party, we had my parents' fiftieth wedding anniversary celebration on my front lawn. I was pleased my brother and sister agreed to have it there instead of the small place where we all had lived for so many years, but I was even more pleased that I had somehow brought my new home into my family. I had no idea my family had already been there.

During one of my trips to the Kentucky State Archives, I found the land grant Elisha claimed for himself and Haley in 1873. When he left Grassy, he sold the grant to Haley's family where it eventually passed on to a childless nephew who is buried in a small cemetery on that land a hundred yards from my house. The land no longer meant anything for Elisha; no land meant anything to him, except for a small plot overlooking Greasy Creek and Hopkins Creek, the two creeks where he was once happy and where he still rests.

By World War I, most of Elisha's contemporaries were gone; the old soldiers, who were once young men imbued with fire, were gone as well. In the rush to find graves for the Spanish Influenza victims, many of their grave markers, rude crosses or simple field rocks, were pushed aside and their graves were lost forever.

Joseph Hopkins' bones may be lost, but I suspect they rest under one of three beautifully cut and inexplicably unmarked stones in the family plot of Doctor Joshua Gore in Bloomfield, Nelson County, Kentucky, just behind the church where Joseph's funeral was preached after his execution. Joshua Gore was a surgeon for the fabled Kentucky Orphan Brigade, commanded by John Cabell Breckinridge, who was the last commander of Joseph Hopkins. Gore would have given a final resting place to a Confederate soldier who was shot down for something he did not do, especially if that soldier was captured in service to the great commander he once served. The stones are blank, and not even the descendants of Gore's family know who lies in those three aligned graves, but I am confident Joseph lies there.

Of course, his bones may be near the field where he was executed, and there is an uncomfortable resonance about that place, but it is one of anguish, and not of peace, like what I felt while standing in the Gore plot. If, for some reason, I could someday prove those bones are his, and if I am still walking this earth, I will bring him home to Greasy Creek, to be near the gathered bones of his family.

Could the boys who came back to Greasy Creek have known, before they left, that their world would be irrevocably changed? Could they have known that in the celebration of their departures the funeral of their way of life was also being held? I wonder if there is language enough in this world to express how they felt when they came back and saw their country struggling to mend itself. Their friends were gone, if not taken by disease or bullets, then lost to an undying enmity that would never yield. The family circles they once knew and dreamed of in the glow of a campfire were gone. A brother or a nephew or a cousin, perhaps even a son or a father might be dead or might no longer be welcome, and these former soldiers began new family circles to replace those broken by war.

There were many trees to split new fence rails, as the old ones were now cold ashes from a thousand campfires, but the picturesque fences never returned. The new barbed wire, viciously effective and designed as much to keep visitors out as to keep stock in, became the accepted fencing material and it merely reflected the mistrust of everything that marked human exchange. There were no longer honorable handshakes between men to seal bargains; both sides were too busy looking at their partner's other hand for a gun or a knife. Men retreated to their cabins, and any knock at the door was unexpected and unwanted.

An uneasy slumber fell over the soldiers from Greasy Creek, and few nights passed with the gift of dreamless sleep. With crushing poverty and unceasing fatigue from the memory of what had passed, there was little resistance to the timber speculators who came into the hills with a little hard money, and part of the birthright of their children was sold for a pittance. When the coal speculators came, the rest of it was squandered. Did they know what they were doing, I wondered as I read the deeds in the county courthouse, the deeds that recorded the disintegration of their wealth? Each of my ancestors had given up their coal or timber in book after book, and each document resounded like iron bells at plague time, tolling the losses again and again.

It was the Original Sin for Greasy Creek, for Pike County, for all the coal rich counties of eastern Kentucky; the sins of the fathers visited upon the sons and their sons forever. The impermeable stain on the land where I grew up, it broke the bond that once existed between the pioneers and the wilderness that sustained them. It shattered the contract that provided simply that man would live on the land, be nurtured by it, and in return, watch over it and protect it.

But I do not harbor resentment for their folly, if that is what it was. They were broken, whether Union or Confederate, and by the end of the Nineteenth Century, they could scarcely remember the bright hopes their land once offered them. A century later, the final injustice, strip mining, now desecrates their land like nothing imaginable to the progenitors of my race, but in 1900 they could not have envisioned what was to come. They could not, or would not, remember what had passed.

No longer was there reason for the soldiers or their families to remember, to savor any dreams from a long-dead past when they awakened from their fitful sleep. The ebullience of a young country, of pioneers in a wilderness they rose to conquer, of men who were larger than the mountains that could not subdue them, was gone. The heart of their simple childhood was forever stilled. The ethos of a people, the better part of all they believed in, Union or Confederate, had vanished, and only dust remained of their dreams.

Like the aftermath of an invasion of thieves, who took everything that was precious and pure and defiled all that was left, the heart of their being was forfeit. The recent past was unspeakable and the older past too hurtful to remember because it was unrecoverable. In an age of cruel uncertainty, there was agreement only in that there could never be a return to what once was. Their fathers, their sons, their brothers, the women they loved, the promise of hope: mislaid, forgotten, lost in a mindless fury and a following silence too stunning to understand.

And all the geese were gone.

The Beekeeper's Children

Living in the mountains of Eastern Kentucky in late summer is almost an aquatic experience; great waves of humidity replace the breeze that steadily dies off as the summer wanes and air conditioners strain to battle the heat that accompanies it. It was still early as I plunged up the road to the Old Prater to meet a jail crew that was to clear the cemetery for me, but the leaves still dripped from the night's dew and splashed through my partly-opened window as I brushed them. During the short drive from Grassy Creek to Greasy Creek I noticed my Jeep was yet covered with condensate and even the half-hour of highway speed had not blown it dry. I still had my wipers on as the Old Prater came into view.

The boys had their weed-cutters out of the jailer's van before I came to a stop, and were attacking the overgrown road to the Old Prater with the enthusiasm only prisoners on work release would have. I could hear them swearing and good-naturedly needling each other as they began to slash through the year's undergrowth, threatening each other with their noisy machines:

"Hey, jerk," one said. "Watch what you're doin'. You could've cut off my pussy finger!"

"Hell, boy, you're in jail. You ain't got no need for it, anyway," his assailant laughed.

I smiled as I listened to their scatological badinage. They are grateful for any break from the monotony of jail, I concluded, even if it were merely a temporary discharge into the

151

oppressive heat of July in the mountains. They had their work cut out for them this time; the Old Prater was running riot with weeds and chiggers, and it had never been an easy job to keep clean.

When Rissie was still alive, my brother bought two gentle goats to keep the weeds down and, for the time they were there, the cemetery was cleaner than it had ever been. The goats nibbled delicately around the gravestones, and the grass was smooth and uniform. It was as if the Old Prater had its own full-time groundskeeper to keep even the most innocuous weed from trespassing on its graves. And they were precise in their work. Even when my brother brought feed and water to them in the evenings, they were deliberate in running toward him, and dashed around the graves like lithe runners across an obstacle course.

Paul had brought the goats to the cemetery after Jim Prater refused him permission to use chemicals to kill weeds. It might make his cattle sick, he said. We were all familiar with Jim's cattle. In contrast to the goats' subtle dances between the stones, his cattle had some uncanny ability to unchain the cemetery gate and admit themselves to a clumsy revel that always resulted in the need to reset the markers, especially Hester's marble spire.

But the goat experiment lasted less than a season. One day, as Paul was trudging up the hill with their rations, they did not rush to him. He did not see them meandering around the cemetery as they usually did, and they did not come to him when he called. When he opened the gate, he found one already dead and the other jerking in its death throes, its kidneys shut down from the poison coursing through its veins. When it died, Paul found their water bowls half-filled with green antifreeze.

He burned them on the cemetery where they served, and he did not bring goats back to the Old Prater. We began the human job of cutting weeds and clearing the graves once more. Again, only human effort was enlisted to keep the cemetery presentable.

I remembered those goats as I watched the jailbirds as they avidly, if not artfully, began their work. These young men were barely more than boys and not hardened criminals. Minor offenders, their crimes were drinking up, or smoking up, their paychecks instead of making child support payments or, for the same reason, were unable to pay a DUI fine. They reminded me of giant, angry carpenter bees, chewing into the under-growth as single-mindedly as the real ones that regularly attacked my house in spite of the insecticide I sprayed on it every year.

I was also reminded that real bees were rarely to be found on Greasy Creek anymore and not just because the general bee population across the country was down from the mite epidemic. There were simply fewer people with the time or the patience to take care of bees and rob the hives for their treasure, especially on Greasy Creek where government checks made it much easier to buy a plastic squeeze bottle of Sue Bee Honey from South Dakota instead.

Once, nearly every house on Greasy had at least one stand of whitewashed hives behind it, ready to supply the home it served with "sweetening." And there was always an old man with netted hat and large, kindly hands, gently smoking his tiny workers, brushing them easily away from the combs, and removing the rich, yellow confection of a season of tulip poplar blooms. All the while, the family waited for their grandfather to return with his riches, with biscuits browning in the oven and chicken turning golden in the pan above it.

At least it seemed that way to me, for Frank Hopkins was among the best of the beekeepers of Greasy Creek, and was visited frequently for advice on how best to deal with a swarm or how to keep intruders out of the hives.

"Don't hurt them bees," he would tell us every May as we began to again clear away the clover on the Old Prater for Memorial Day. "You hurt them bees and you won't get no honey for your Mamaw's biscuits." That was a credible threat: there were always dinner buckets of food the women prepared for the workers at that annual chore, and Frank's honey was highly prized.

Frank had joined his first wife on the Old Prater nearly thirty years before this day, after fifty years without her, and there were neither his gentle admonitions to watch for the bees, nor bees themselves to watch out for this year. And it was July instead of May, and Pike County jail prisoners were cleaning the cemetery this year competing for a taste of freedom, instead of my great-grandfather Harrison's children dreaming of a taste of honey in compensation for their labor.

Their unarmed guard came over to me when I exited my Jeep and we walked into the Old Prater for my instructions on where to mow.

"It's a mess, isn't it?" I asked him.

"Well, I've seen worse," he replied. "But not much worse."

Although the custom had always been to clean the cemetery for Decoration Day and the attendant family reunion, there had been no family reunion this year. I did not know that last year's small gathering had been the last, for next year the bulldozers would be covering the small sheaf of land beside the creek where the reduced family would come together. There were simply too many responsibilities elsewhere, with the family growing older, closing with death so frequently in Akron or Louisville or other big cities and I had heard of no one coming back to Greasy Creek for the spring reunion. Unable to find the time to clean the cemetery myself, or to find someone to do it for pay, I accepted the offer of the Pike County jailer who had work-release inmates willing to do the job. So the Old Prater got its annual cleaning in 2002 belatedly, with strangers among the headstones of my family.

I felt no small shame in that.

And if that were not enough to darken my perspective, I had another, more pressing chore: after instructing the prisoners on where to point their Weedeaters, I was leaving for Akron for Caudill Robinson's funeral. He had died the previous day.

I visited him a few weeks before and his physical decline was painfully obvious. Like my father as the end approached, he was resigned to his fate, but still cheerful and oblivious to the attention he was getting.

His sisters fluttered protectively around him and tried to get him to eat, to put some weight back on the tiny frame that was disappearing in front of them.

"Try this, Caudill," they would say. "It's really, really good."

"Well, if it's so God damn good you eat it." And then he would grin and take a small bite just to satisfy them.

While we were sitting in his living room, we talked about the old days on Greasy Creek and, of course, about my father.

"Yeah," he told me, "I can see Marvin in you more and more every day."

I could see parts of Uncle Will's gentle smile as he spoke.

"I think I'm just getting old, Caudill," I replied. "But I appreciate the compliment."

"You know," he replied. "That's the way I look at it. Nothing would please me more than to hear someone say I looked like my dad."

Indeed he resembled Uncle John when he was younger, but actually he looked more like Aunt Bessie. John had been gone for almost as long as Rissie and was buried on Harmon's cemetery near his brother Caudill who had died in the Greasy Creek mine. The older Caudill was John's hero and he never recovered from losing his brother. Bessie agreed with John that they would name their first son after him. Caudill never knew the uncle he had been named for, but Bessie kept his memory alive for her children.

Bessie was as sweet and loving as her brother Jesse was cantankerous and contrary. She had lived a long life, and I hoped she would be all right when I got there.

I also hoped her memory would still include me, for she had transferred to me part of the love she had for Marvin when her sister Rissie took him to raise nearly eight decades before. Marvin, for all the tragedies that had befallen him before he even learned to speak, was loved by Harrison's children as few orphans could have ever hoped to be. With Frank lost in an unfathomable abyss and Rissie a young mother taking the most awesome chore of her life, the other Hopkins girls, Alice, Stella, and Bessie, felt a responsibility to help with Marvin's raising. Bessie, who had not yet begun her own family, fell in love with Marvin much as Rissie had. And since half of Harrison's children were buried near him, I suspect that was why my father felt such a responsibility to the Old Prater.

Bessie would not be buried near her father, however; she would be buried with her husband, but only a stone's throw away in Harmon Robinson's cemetery, where Elisha and Sally's son's tall stone towered over all his children's. This hierarchy was common to mountain cemeteries; that is, a patriarch would be buried and then his children would be buried near him and then their children until succeeding generations lost touch with the custom or the cemetery filled up. On the Old Prater, there were two such hierarchies, with the Praters buried near Ezekiel, the progenitor of the line, and the Hopkins buried near Harrison. But I knew Harrison was not the first Hopkins to be buried there, as surely as I knew my grandfather was the last to take his place near him.

Frank and Jesse had their places near their father. Bud, the oldest, was buried just up the creek, but left three of his own sons to be guarded by his father's shade. Willy, another son, was not buried on Greasy Creek proper, although he slept only a few miles away with his own family. The other boys Harrison raised, Elisha's boys, were not buried on the Old Prater either. Hooker was buried in Floyd County, Paris in a military cemetery in Tennessee, and Uncle Will slept beside his father in that desecrated grave on Ripley Knob. The irony was not lost at family reunions that Harrison's nephews, who thought of him as their father in so many ways, were also his uncles, since Elisha's last wife was Harrison's sister-in-law.

Of Harrison's girls, only Alice, called Big Sis, slept near her father. Stella, after a destructive first marriage and a childless but happy second, slept by her husband, a Hamlin of my mother's family, in another ancient cemetery just up the creek from her brother Bud. Rissie, who had reserved a place for herself beside Harlan, her greatest love after Marvin, slept alone on her property in the old Greasy Creek camp, the same property Harrison's mother lived on before the mines came. That left only Bessie and when she died, she would not be buried near Harrison. If there was anything good about moving the Old Prater to the cemetery where my father was buried, it was that my father would rest near his father. Unfortunately, now Bessie would not be buried close to her father; and sadly, none of her children would be buried near her.

Bessie was in her mid-nineties now, and was the last person in my family to have drawn breath at the same time as Elisha Hopkins. Bessie lived in Ohio with her children, and had buried her husband, a daughter, and would now be burying her oldest son.

On occasion, I would ask her about the family, but did not inquire much about Harrison, mistakenly thinking his illegitimacy would have some bearing on her memory of him. Although that memory now came and went, I hoped she would still be able to tell me something of the past, and something of Elisha, the grandfather of so many on Greasy Creek, and the man whose irrepressible ghost had walked through my dreams since the death of my father.

For a tiny woman, Bessie was remarkably strong. She still had most of her teeth, she told me, in spite of having "all those children," and all the pain she had suffered throughout her life. And she had lived longer than most Hopkins were expected to, eluding death as it called, again and again, on the people she loved.

It was Bessie who told me who Harrison's real father was. I had never wanted to know when I was younger, resenting the man who left my great-grandfather to fend for himself with his cleft palate and the derision of Elisha who wanted only strong sons. But the issue was more complicated than that. Harrison's father was Francis Marion Ratliff, who lived near Dorcus in the 1870 census, but had a legitimate family and, I thought, no contact with his other offspring. As usual, I was wrong.

Francis Marion was known as Frank or Red Ratliff, due to his red hair, which still appears every now and then in the

Hopkins ranks, and Harrison named his first son for his father. Harrison himself was named for Frank's father, and in another one of the great ironies I found as I began my research, I discovered the grave of my great-great grandfather, Francis Marion Ratliff, next to Charlene's great-great grandfather in another mountain hollow, where Francis moved when he left Greasy Creek.

Marion was also my father's birth name, but Rissie changed it to Marvin, perhaps because of her prerogative as his new mother or possibly as an indication that she was not as close to their grandfather as her brother was.

But it never really mattered what his name was; Harrison's family became his extended family, and Bessie always considered herself more than merely my aunt. Often when we talked, she would take the maternal third person and refer to herself as Mamaw. It was obvious she loved my father; her favorite stories were of Marvin, and how he loved to eat, and how she loved to cook for him. After three-quarters of a century, she still delighted in remembering him smile.

"He scared Rissie to death," she told me, "when he got his first car."

"What was it, Aunt Bess?" I asked her.

"I don't remember," she said, laughingly. "Some old blue Plymouth with red wheels. He put Rissie in it and took off a'flyin' up the road. When they came back, she said she'd never ride with him again. 'Course she did. She'd do anything for Marvin."

But there were other stories of harder times; perhaps they made the good times more piquant; perhaps there were too many of them not to relate to me, as if she were afraid I would mistakenly assume that life was all good back then. Perhaps she wanted me to understand life's joys are always tempered by life's cruelties.

In November 1918, news of the Armistice in Europe reached Greasy Creek. Bessie was ecstatic; her brothers had gone to fight Kaiser Bill and were somewhere across the water, but now they would be coming home. She had followed the war news on a big map on the classroom wall at Middle Greasy School, as their teacher read from the newspapers and struggled with the strange names that appeared to her: *the Argonne, Chateau-Thierry, Belleau Wood.* She had joined in the pledge to the flag with her classmates, and she remembered where the boys who would never come home had once sat, or where they had played on the field which still resonated with the echoes of their childhood laughter.

For some reason, school had been closed recently, and when her father gave her the good news, she wanted to run down the hollow to Harmon's house, where his son Johnny, her grinning sweetheart lived. But her mother would not let her go.

"We're all going down there tomorrow," Lila said. "You can tell him then."

The next day Bessie put on her best clothes, the ones her mother had washed and ironed the night before, and the family walked down the twisting wagon road to the forks of Greasy Creek where the Robinsons lived. There was a crowd on the front porch, and she could hear singing inside the house, but her mother would not let her go in.

"Why not?" she asked. "I want to see Johnny."

"Just wait," her mother said, and Harrison and his family, all dressed in their Sunday clothes, stood outside in the November chill until the singing stopped.

In a few minutes, Bessie saw her Johnny, but if he saw her, he said nothing. He was silent, although his eyes were red-rimmed and glazed. Although he was only a few years older than she was, he was a pallbearer and was helping the older men carry a coffin out of the house. Four coffins that came out of Harmon's rambling house that day, one for Johnny's older sister Emma and her infant child, and three more, one for each of her other three children. They had all died of Spanish Influenza, which was ravaging the entire country, and seemed to choose only the healthiest, or those with the brightest promise, as victims.

Bessie was heartbroken that she could not comfort the boy she would someday marry, but only pallbearers were allowed to go up to Harmon's family cemetery with the body. It was against the law to have a big funeral in Kentucky then.

Not long afterward, Johnny felt equally impotent as he stood on the path to the Old Prater as Bessie followed her mother's coffin, sadly pantomiming the march Johnny had performed only a few months before.

I wondered if Bessie knew then that she would not be buried on the Old Prater, for she knew she would be a wife and would be buried beside her husband. And in the custom of the day, he would be buried near his father. Harrison, of course, could not be buried near his father; he had only his mother and a brother to be buried near, and they were buried elsewhere. So again the question arose: Why had he selected the Old Prater for his burying grounds, if no other Hopkins was buried there first?

Aunt Bessie told me that Dorcus, Harrison's mother, was not buried on the Old Prater and neither was Harrison's brother after he drowned in the river near the mill that was grinding his corn. It was unexpected, for Joe was considered an excellent swimmer, and the family often wondered if there was some foul play involved in his death, but I suspect it was just another tragic accident, a story like a hundred others that could be told on any Greasy Creek cemetery.

Caudill once told me the family ghost stories about Joe. It seems that after he drowned, his clothes were hung out to dry on a fence as the women washed his body and clothed him in his Sunday best. The night after the funeral, the family heard something knocking in the house, and followed the sound to the trunk where Joe's death clothes had been folded. Opening the trunk, they found nothing, but the knocking returned. They opened the trunk again and still found nothing.

Dorcus knew what she had to do. His clothes still had mud on them from the river, she said. They had not been cleaned before they were put away. She would wash and iron them and Joe would be satisfied. This she did, and the knocking stopped.

Did that really happen? In the cold logic of daytime, I would say no, of course. Ghost stories have been made up to frighten children into sleep since the beginnings of human record, and all the witnesses to this event were gone, as was the trunk. So there is no forensic evidence; in fact, there are few artifacts of the old days in the Hopkins family. I asked if anyone knew what happened to Dorcus' trunk, but no one did.

When Frank died, Laura gave me the old steamer trunk he kept in the only built-in closet in their house as long as he lived. I had seen it in the "press" many times, but was never allowed to open it. It contained bits and pieces of his life with Ethel; some of her clothes, her childhood dolls, postcards from France, and a tiny box with a piece of tissue paper inside with these words: "Coins that covered Warren G's eyes." The box was empty. I wondered if that trunk may have been Harrison's, or possibly Dorcus' before, but I suspect Frank had bought it for his wife and Dorcus' trunk went up in the conflagration Pearl rendered for her wayward husband.

Neither could I find any record of children of Joseph and his wife Arminta, and I could not find any trace of her after his death. No remarriage, no land transactions, nothing. Perhaps she died when she heard the news, sank down in grief and was buried with her young husband, but no one knew. Just another lost grave; another bit of Greasy Creek history that will remain unknown and unknowable.

I knew only what Aunt Bessie told me: that Dorcus had forbidden Harrison to bury his brother on the Old Prater, or her either when she passed away. They were both buried on another Robinson Cemetery on Greasy Creek, where their graves had been obliterated, just as most of the small Samuel Robinson Cemetery had been. I knew that little cemetery had filled up soon after the Civil War, but the cemetery where Dorcus was buried, and where her grave was lost to a bulldozer clearing out a site for a dog pen, is still accepting burials.

But the Old Prater was young when Dorcus died; there was plenty of space. Why had she eschewed burial on the hillside where Harrison placed his wife, and where later he would rest, and ultimately, most of his children? Again, I wished I had talked to the elders of my family more when I was younger. I had no proof of who was buried in the unmarked graves on the Old Prater, and the lower cemetery, where I knew some of my family was buried, was even more of a mystery.

The refusal of the KYDOT to offer me any assistance in finding and identifying graves on the lower cemetery had caused me to abandon my effort to learn more about it, but I still fought with them over the Old Prater. Nearly five years had passed since I first asked them for a forensic anthropologist. I considered it a simple request, one in accordance with law, but what greeted me was official stonewalling, typical of the way Eastern Kentuckians were customarily treated. It is a common perception of Eastern Kentuckians that their state neglects them; almost as if Frankfort had written off our region, consigning it to the coal industry for "development." That simply meant the mountains would be ground into moonscapes by the great earth-moving machines that regularly pushed thousands of tons of rock and dirt off mountaintops and into the valleys, just to get at the thin coal seams that snaked along the mountain ridges.

In fact, I was first told that no services could be rendered the Old Prater at all since there was no tombstone predating the 1911 implementation of a statewide vital statistics system in Kentucky.

"But there are," I told them. "Ezekiel Prater and Henry D. Adkins both died before 1910 and their tombstones have no date because Union Civil War stones had only the deceased's name, company, and regiment."

That surprised them. *OK, we'll get back to you.*

And they did, but with another excuse. This time I was told that services could be rendered only if the cemetery qualified for inclusion on the National Register of Historic Places. And what did that entail, I asked, although I already knew. After dealing with the KYDOT's intransigence, I flirted briefly with nominating the cemetery myself, and reviewed the rules for inclusion. I thought the cemetery would easily qualify, but if I were the one to prevent the cemetery from being moved, I would forever be blamed for keeping the cemetery inaccessible for the families who might go there if it were in a different location. So when the KYDOT came up with this one, I let matters take their own course.

An archaeologist came up from Frankfort to check out the cemetery. He was surly and resentful for having to waste his time going over what already had been declared of no historic value, according to a survey commissioned by the KYDOT to one of its subcontractors. He brought no camera to photograph the tombstones, and did not have even a notepad in his pocket to jot down any pertinent information.

But when we arrived at the cemetery, after listening to my recitation of the cemetery's history during the half-hour drive to it, he was more subdued. And when we entered the cemetery, his eyes widened. He dropped down to look at Zeke's stone, then Henry D's and began scrambling from tombstone to tombstone, jotting down notes on whatever scrap of paper he could find.

He had little to say as we left, except to ask me to clarify some historical points I had made on the trip up.

When I later asked for his report from the KYDOT, they told me he was no longer an employee.

How typical, I thought. You fired his ass because of his report.

They also said that an independent consultant had been hired to make a review. When that report came back, it was even more positive.

Since the KYDOT could not deny now the Old Prater was historic, they agreed to assign me an archaeologist. The cemetery did qualify for inclusion on the National Register, and it would still be moved, but it would be treated appropriately.

I was satisfied, and although there was still no consideration of the seven graves on the mournful Samuel Robinson Cemetery, as the lower cemetery was now referred to by the KYDOT, I took what I could get. Samuel Robinson and his daughter had come to Pike County as escapees from the genocide President Andrew Jackson had wrought on the Cherokee nation. I could prove that, but it had no impact on the KYDOT, especially since his grave had been obliterated, along with at least a dozen others. I was grateful just to get help on the Old Prater.

While I was furiously researching every lead for possibilities as to who was buried on my cemetery, the KYDOT was just as furiously purchasing all the property surrounding it to take ownership of the cemetery and begin its removal. I was working under a Damoclean sword and I was curious that nothing had been done for years now since all the surrounding property had been bought up and the process of removing houses had already begun.

The KYDOT had a problem: they now effectively owned the cemetery and, as a result of my insistence, it was going on the National Register. For the average landowner, that presents no problem, as he is encouraged to preserve the property but has no real restrictions on its use. For a public entity, it is a different story: the state could still move the cemetery, but would have to observe strict archaeological guidelines. Neither could they abandon the cemetery, for as a National Register property, they would have to maintain it forever. When they confirmed I would be getting an archaeologist, I knew the fight was over and I could sleep easily now for the first time in years.

There was some good to come of my aggravation: for fear of losing forever the graves of family members I never knew existed, I plunged into the work the state should have done, and the things I learned, I would have never learned otherwise.

I now knew Dorcus was not buried on the Old Prater because it had passed into the hands of Ezekiel Prater, whose regiment, the 39th Kentucky Mounted Infantry, the same regiment that had fought the 10th Kentucky Cavalry, Joseph's regiment, at Saltville. This had no bearing on Zeke; he had nothing to do with Joseph's capture, and would not have forbidden a Reb to be buried on his property, but it was too much for Dorcus, whose bitterness ran deep.

But Harrison did not share in that acrimony, oddly enough because his mother protected him from it. Indeed, he began his family plot on the Old Prater instead of beside his mother in spite of his love for her. Harrison had more than enough turmoil in his life and when his time came, the memories he kept of a kindly old man and a simpler time lured him back to the Old Prater.

Cornelius Hopkins married Dorcus Thacker in Patrick County, Virginia in 1812. Ten years later, he set out with a land grant for Pike County, Kentucky, which bordered Virginia, and had just been carved out of Floyd County. He went alone and tamed the wilderness he found there, at least enough to make it safe for his family. In 1824, he returned to Patrick County, sold his seventy-two acres to his brother James, and brought his wife and four children back to their new home. There he had at least three more children I knew of, and lived out his long, rich life, escaping tragedy until the War came.

His sons and daughters had their own family cemeteries up and down the creek, but no one knew where he and Dorcus were buried. Now I had discovered their plots, in a bare spot that an old wire fence once surrounded in the middle of the Old Prater Cemetery.

Hooker Prater was probably right; the plot could have held more than four graves. Now, at least, the archaeologist would tell me enough to help me identify my ancestors.

My theory made sense, and the family agreed with me, but we did not know what would come out of those graves. We hoped the ground was not so acidic that there would be nothing there but the residual black dirt, that their bodies would have been buried deep enough in pH-neutral clay that not everything would have dissolved into dust. But we did not have great hopes; they had been there nearly a century and a half.

When Cornelius and Dorcus died, sometime between 1870 and 1880, the plot was on the property of Matilda and Samuel Robinson. It would have been perfectly situated in a small cove, half-hidden from the valley below, for the two old people to have a modest cabin to live out their final days.

Cornelius was in his nineties when his granddaughter Dorcus presented him with Harrison. Although I had nothing more than a hint here or a possibility there, everything fell into place so perfectly, I knew my theory had to be correct. When the graves were opened, I would know for sure.

In the 1860 census, Cornelius and Dorcus lived at the mouth of the creek, near the river, but by 1870, they had moved to where the Old Prater now stood. It was safer deep within the hollow, especially for someone who had a Confederate son.

In the 1870 census, Cornelius is listed as ninety years old, and his wife Dorcus Thacker Hopkins, for whom Harrison's mother was named, is listed as sixty-five. I suspect she was older, for their Virginia marriage license was dated 1812, and seven years old would have been too young for even a pioneer bride. So she was closer to seventy-five; but after a lifetime of unimaginable toil, had the right to some small vanity.

Both Cornelius and Dorcus are gone by the 1880 census, and church records indicate their daughter Matilda was one of the first members of the Greasy Creek Regular Baptist Church, formed in 1871. I suspect she helped found the church to bring some comfort to her aging parents, who were now too old to make the rigorous journey to neighboring creeks where churches that had survived the War held services. I further suspect the first meeting place for the circuit rider was Cornelius and Dorcus' cabin.

Also in the 1870 census, Cornelius is listed as "laborer," but what kind of labor could a ninety-year old man do? Could he yet fell trees, and clear off land for pastures? Could he break new ground, and drive teams through the fields, or plow corn on stifling summer days when the humidity blocked any cooling of his near century-old frame? Probably not, but could he not yet tend bees? He had survived the wilderness, had seen a country rise on the shores of the New World, and had watched as another country was nearly born from the womb of the first one, and if he had learned anything, it was patience.

Rissie told me once that Harrison taught Frank to raise bees, and Frank loved them. He continued raising them even after a swarm he was attempting to coax into a hive from a buckeye tree fell on him, nearly stinging him to death. Rissie said that it was late summer and the creek was nearly dry, but Frank ran to it desperately searching for enough water to dive under to escape the angry cloud upon him. For a week, he shivered and sweated, in agony from hundreds of bee stings, going in and out of consciousness. The preachers were called to "try on him," since faith healing was free and the family was too poor to afford doctors.

But at last he recovered, and after a few weeks, went back to his "beegums." He could barely walk without help, but his only concern was that the hives had not been timely robbed. He was not angry at the bees, Rissie told me. They were doing nothing more than protecting their queen, and he understood their anger. Or perhaps he loved the bees his father had given him because they were his fathers', and possibly Cornelius' before him.

Only a gentle spirit like Harrison could endure the occasional sting without flinching, to grieve for the tiny creature that doomed itself when it struck him. And only a truly gentle spirit would be brave enough to open an angrily buzzing hive to inspect its production without fear.

Frank learned to love his bees from his father, but from whom did Harrison get his love? Not from his mother Dorcus, for beekeeping was not woman's work then, as it would be even less likely to be today. And not from Elisha, who was not a gentle man, and who scorned his grandson with the incomplete face, with the language unintelligible to him because there was no roof in Harrison's mouth with which words could be easily formed. Perhaps Harrison learned from his father, but I doubted Frank Ratliff could have spared the time from his legitimate family to teach his wood's colt son the arcane science of keeping bees.

It had to have been Cornelius, who unequivocally loved the sickly child his granddaughter brought him. Cornelius, I somehow knew, saw the hypocrisy of Elisha's scolding Dorcus for having illegitimate children when he already had three families and would eventually take another. Cornelius would have known that the boy needed a skill, some tool he could master and have for his own when he faced the world of men. And he would have taught Harrison that craft. The buzzing of the jailbirds' machines did not drown out the voices I heard as I saw another scene play out before me.

"Come on, little boy," the old man says. "Let's go get your Maw some honey." And the ruined mouth of the child, with no complete sphincter with which to close his lips, spread widely, joyously, as he followed the old man onto the hillside where the buzzing hives rested.

"Remember, son," he says. "Always take care of the bees."

And the child replies: "Alhays hake care ah the hees."

"These bees are your bees; if I ain't here, your Uncle Lum will take care of them until you get old enough."

"Uncle Hun?"

Lum was Columbus Christopher Hopkins, late of the 39th Kentucky Mounted Infantry USA, the same regiment that most of the Pike County boys joined when they took the Northern side. Cornelius had not seen either his Union son or his Confederate son much during the War, and he would not see his Confederate boy alive again.

Elisha had brought his parents to the forks of Greasy when life worsened during the War and he had to move them away from danger, from their homestead down on the river. While the conflict was raging, Elisha helped his father with the bees, but only because there was no one else to help. Now that Columbus was home, Elisha gave him the job. Elisha enjoyed producing a different type of nectar.

Columbus had not gone with the troops to Saltville; it was a good thing. If he fought there, he could not have come home to face Elisha's wrath. It was difficult enough to face his father, who knew Columbus' regiment was part of the Hadean legion that fought and captured Joseph and guarded him on the way to his doom. And although he knew his Union service was right, it was a constant torment for him that his brother had taken the other course, and had died defending what he thought was right.

Lum worked constantly, sweating to cleanse himself, searching for something to accomplish, something to do just to get his mind off the War and the destruction it wrought on his family. It was no chore to help with the bees. He told his father he would husband them for Harrison as long as it took, and if the little boy survived childhood, as Elisha said he would not, then he would give him the bees when he was man enough to care for them.

What made me see these scenes, beginning with Joseph and Elisha on Ripley Knob? What human CRT in the back of my brain flashed these images to my eyes? What made these stories, so clear from opening scene to dénouement, reveal themselves to me? I could not explain it, and would not mention them to others. Already, my family wondered if my work had become an obsession, as indeed it had. I had made a commitment: what I could not do for my father, when I was powerless to prevent his death, I resolved I would do for his family. Perhaps it was not obsession at all; perhaps it was more in the realm of possession. *But by what, or whom, I wondered?*

Perhaps I was cracking up. There could not have been a spectral voice on the Old Prater when I stood there, alone, and heard Elisha's name whispered to me. I hated my great-great-great grandfather, whom I never knew, for the way he treated Harrison, whom I also never knew, but whom I loved as my father did, as did my grandfather, and as everyone who ever knew him did. Harrison was the antithesis to Elisha, everyone agreed.

"Lord, how mean that man was to Paw," the family would say.

"What would he do?" I would ask.

"Anything mean," they would answer. "He never had a good word for him."

But of course, their stories were relayed to me third-hand, since they had received them second-hand. I wondered how true they were. There was Uncle Will, who had only one request at his death, that he be taken to Ripley Knob to be buried next to his father. He had to have loved Elisha. Why, I asked myself?

It came to me as I cleared the few weeds that grew around Harrison's grave before the jailbirds reached his plot. Even though I had not cleaned the whole cemetery that year, I had kept the Hopkins family graves clear of weeds with my visits over the previous five, and his grave was remarkably clean. I sat down near him, and in my mind formed a question: *Did you ever forgive Elisha, Paw?*

I knew he did, somehow.

I knew there was a final scene in Elisha's life, and only Harrison and Dorcus were privy to it. Somehow I could see it too, as if I had been there, as if I were an ember glowing on the hearth Elisha built for Mary in that cabin up on Ripley, and I watched the act play out for my benefit.

I suspect that scene had been revealed to Hooker as well, on those lonely nights he sat here, or slept here, looking for the grave of his lost child. He must have seen it, as I was seeing it now:

Alone on a bed in the second room of the cabin he built on Ripley Knob to escape life in the valley down below, Elisha stares at the fire. Dorcus enters the room and removes the great black bonnet she has worn since Joseph drowned. She lights her pipe with a wooden shaving Mary keeps in a cup on the mantelpiece. Elisha stares at her as she puffs on her pipe before sitting in a rocking chair near the bed. She stares back, and Elisha looks away as she finally speaks.

"You know what I'm going to say now, don't you?" she asks. "Listen to me, Lige. Listen to me, you old fool. It's time to talk."

Elisha turns his back to her, to the daughter who has stood by him all these years, the daughter who gave him no legitimate grandchildren, but who bore the millstone of his anger, his grief, and the destitution of his losses and still loved him.

"You ain't got much time left and I don't neither. I'm taking the boys off of this damn hill with me. They're going to live with Harrison in his place. You can come if you want to, or lay up here and rot for all I care."

Elisha says nothing, but he turns to his daughter with the remnant of the awful glare he once reserved for his enemies.

"You ain't takin my boys, Sister," he says deliberately.

"Indeed I am, old man. It ain't healthy up here, and Mary's agreed."

The great heart that sustained him through unfathomable times can no longer raise him from his bed and his glare softens.

"You know it's time for them to go, Lige. But you got somethin' to say to Harrison 'afore we leave here or I'm takin' the whole damn crowd with me tonight, Mary included."

Elisha's nostrils, hidden in the white forest of his beard, flare at the mention of Harrison's name, but then he softens. Has it come to this, he wonders? He knows what Dorcus wants and knows what he must do; yet he will not give in.

I don't know if I want to be redeemed, he thinks.

"That boy has a fine family, and they all love him like there ain't no tomorrow. And it's time you admit that, unless you want to spend eternity in hell, which you know you very well deserve."

She pauses to let her words sink in, and his white beard moves as he grinds his teeth, searching for a response.

"You can't live forever, Paw. You're sick. Your heart's wore out."

Elisha says nothing, but knows she is telling the truth. He knows his time will soon be exhausted on this earth; too many vague mists have flown past his window lately, too many half-formed shapes from a past he struggles to forget, or perhaps to remember. Of late, he has attempted both. And he has had visitors, spirits in the guise of owls, deer, mourning doves; specters, he knows, warning him to prepare, warning him his time is near.

"Everbody's gone, Paw," she continues.

171

"Joe's gone, Lige, Zach too. Mommy and Sally are gone."
And finally: " So's Haley."
She continues to press her case:
"I thought nothing could hurt me like it did when Uncle Joe was killed, and then when my Joe drowned, it tore my heart out. I'm tellin' you this because you're my daddy, and I don't want to see you in your grave knowin' you never made peace with the best man that ever walked this creek."

She gives him no chance for rebuttal; she hammers the lesson she learned long before he did, and his eyes soften even more.

"'Bout everbody but you and me is gone now, old man. I ain't gonna tell you what to say, but you gotta say it. And you're gonna say it tonight."

It is his last chance for redemption, for cleansing, and it takes the daughter who was stronger than all his sons to make him do it.

His lips are dry and parched. Like grave dust, he thinks. And no water, no whiskey, nothing that flows of this earth can wet them.

Finally, he finds the power to speak: "All right, Sister. Tell the boy to come in."

His boys stayed with him until he died a few weeks later, and with his final blessing, moved in with Harrison and his family until they became men. Harrison moved up the creek to build a house where my parents' house now stands, and Dorcus returned to her husband, the only man she ever married, only when she could no longer give birth. Three years later, Harrison buried her next to his brother on the George Robinson Cemetery, down the creek from the Old Prater, and named for the son of Matilda and Samuel.

Harrison would not be buried next to Dorcus. He grew up in her world, but it was not the world he wanted to remember. He had seen destitution and loss from the War, and he had seen the violence and heartbreak that came afterward, when there were still scores to settle and there was only apprehension when hoofbeats were heard in the night.

172

It was different before the War, when Greasy Creek gave its people a harsh but good life. Harrison had heard stories of that halcyon time since childhood, and compared to afterward, when there was no money and no schools and no hope, he chose the former, even if it would appear to him only in his dreams. His final resting-place would be, he thought, like returning to the soft goosedown of his great-grandmother's feather bed. He had never known such a bed since hers, and would never feel that comfort again in his life. He looked forward to that, when he was old and it was his time, after he had raised a family and perfected his line.

Delilafare Riley was Harrison's first and only love. Her father John served in the Confederate Army at the beginning of the War, but later joined the Union, not because he had a change of heart, but because he was realistic enough to know that the Confederacy was too weak to protect its people in Pike County. The border had been closed and armed guards stood at every pass between Kentucky and Virginia, and in Pike County, civil government ceased to exist, leaving its citizens prey to bandits and thieves. Only the Union was strong enough to create a regiment that would protect the people, and John reluctantly signed on.

But that made no never mind, Dorcus told him. John Riley was still a Yankee, and even worse, he went over to become one. And if Harrison trusted the daughter of a turncoat, he was asking for trouble. She would betray him and break his heart, she said. But it broke Dorcus' heart instead when her prophecy came true, when Lila gave herself to another man.

It was not her fault, Lila swore in court when Harrison filed a lawsuit against her seducer. Elisha's response was typical:

"Boy, what are you doing?" Elisha asked him. "You don't law somebody for taking your woman, you blow his God damn brains out! Ain't you got no respect for yourself? It's no man you are; you're a blubbering child."

But Lige was wrong, and before he died, Dorcus made him own up to it, just as she herself had. It took a man to accept what Harrison learned to live with.

Harrison had seen too much violence, and he knew it begot more, and in spite of the humiliation of such a lawsuit, he wanted justice. Some people say he carried a bullet in his back from the days when he was high-strung and ready to fight those who made fun of him, and there were many. But I could not imagine Harrison fighting. He did have tumors on his back, skin cancer for which there was no cure then, and it eventually killed him. But why would anyone want to shoot such a good man? I hoped it was not true.

"Be careful, now," Caudill told me he would say, when Harrison stayed with them and Caudill was allowed to sleep with his grandfather. "Don't hurt Paw's sore back."

But Harrison lived a long life. He had learned to survive, to suckle his mother's breast, and eventually keep in most of the hard food he learned to eat. As he grew older, he learned the ways of men, and attempted to be one of them. He grew a mustache to cover the gap in his upper lip and learned how to force the two sides of his upper lip to form words precisely, if slowly, and made himself understood except when he got excited. That was often, as he was frequently teased, and fought back, taking his early boldness from the near mythical figure of his grandfather Elisha.

Lila changed him; she accepted his deformity for what it was: a mere flaw in the shell of a beautiful soul, and when they began their life together, he knew it would be only her for him as long as he lived. And except for one lapse, it was a good life.

When she told him what she did, his heart crumbled. Now he knew what betrayal meant, and he could feel the blind fury that he always sensed, the anger that was always lingering on Greasy Creek, always waiting release like a penned animal waiting to break free. But he was a Christian in the church Matilda had formed to help heal the wounds that bled all over Greasy Creek, and he was determined not to follow the same path so many others had to early graves and vendettas that never ended.

The courts failed him; Lige told him they would, and he swallowed the bile that rose up in his throat every day as he tried to forgive her.

Another child was born, and then finally the twins, Jesse and Bessie, who were the last children they would have. This is a sign, he thought, something sent to tell me that the past is finally past. It was the final release from the thralldom of her mistake, and he could go to his grave a satisfied man.

But it was Lila who went first.

Death came near in November of 1918 with the Influenza and Lila sickened in the first wave. She did not die, but she was like the other survivors: pale and weak, barely able to stand, let alone do the cooking and cleaning, the woman's work she had done for thirty years for the man who loved her without stipulation.

It was no contest when Death came calling again, only a few months later. Harrison reserved a spot next to her for himself. And he brought a cutting from Dorcus' pink rose bush to plant in front of her stone.

It grew and flourished for fifty years, but as the cemetery fell into neglect, it withered. By the time of the last burial on the Old Prater, it had disappeared.

Harrison never remarried, even though the Old Regulars would have permitted, even expected him to. He had been a good man, they told him, and he deserved a companion, but for him there was only Lila and his children. He would never need anything more.

The next to be buried in the Hopkins plot was Warren G, my father's only blood brother, and the third was Ethel. As the oldest child, Frank had the right to place his family close to his father. And then the tiny man himself, with the great loving heart that exculpated any of his physical shortcomings, took his place beside the woman he loved.

As the years passed, Harrison's family found their way back to the Old Prater, sometimes to bring a child of their own, an infant dead of some arcane disease, or perhaps lost in a fire or from some tragic accident. Harlen, his son-in-law was buried on the hill above him and then Alice came and then Jesse soon after, children again in their coffins, yearning for the peace of being near Harrison. And all would be carried up the hill. Like weary children straggling home at sundown, they came to take their places near their father.

I do not believe they came there strictly out of fealty. There was that custom throughout the mountains, and throughout the world for that matter. In the Old Prater, there were ranks of Praters from Zeke's place westward; three succeeding generations were buried behind his stone.

But there was something more with Harrison and his children. It was as if the man had been so good, so paternally decent that his children sought to leave their own coils or some part of themselves close by to absolve or at least obscure whatever human frailty had marked them in life. And when they were judged, they would have his shade to vouch for them.

And none of them could have conceived that a road would move their cemetery.

Yet it has come to this, I mused, as I headed back into my Jeep for another trek back down the mountain. I had a long trip ahead of me for yet another burial.

For a moment, I considered asking the jail crew to cut down the weeds on the tiny Samuel Robinson Cemetery, the one that Rissie has so fiercely protected during her life. But I knew they would not have found it in the weeds shrouding the seven graves it held, and I said nothing. That much-abused ground had learned to accommodate insults.

This is about all I can do this trip, I thought. I wish I could do more, but it's too late. I wish Harrison could have been buried beside his mother, so I could take her and her drowned son to the new place when I take the rest of the family, but it's too late for that too. I wish she had not been so bitter, and Lige would not have been so bitter, but there is no way that could have been.

If only the War had not poisoned them to the world where Harrison, in spite of his suffering, found peace. If only the War had not come to Greasy Creek.

But it did. It surely did. To a quiet place where life played out its simple masques with a grace that could never be recaptured, to a home where hearts had never been bereft of comfort or love.

Harrison knew such a place existed, because his great-grandfather had told him so, because his great-grandmother wrapped him in goosedown, and sang softly to him, and rocked him by the firelight.

On a clear spring day, when the War was long over, and the hives needed repair from the winter, Cornelius looked up from his work to see Joseph walking toward him, grinning like he did when he was a boy. Unbelieving, and on trembling legs, the old man ran to clutch him, hold him close again and after a while they walked off the hill and down into the valley. They were not noticed as they passed the houses where the women were cooking dinner, passed the field where plowmen were laying off the fields, passed the creek where children were chasing minnows among the stones. No one saw them, save for Elisha's horses, which whinnied and snorted in protest at the men who were beginning a journey without them.

Not long afterward the elder Dorcus, now too old to rock a child, spoke to her husband and her second son as they called on her in her sleep, and did not awaken again on this earth.

At the elder Dorcus' funeral, while the congregation sang the mournful hymns they were compelled to sing at such times, and Cornelius' bees worked the clover above his grave, the younger Dorcus rocked her fitful son to sleep. She sang softly to him, under her breath so no one would hear, afraid the memories her grandparents gave him might be pried out of his heart by funerals. There had been too many and she would not have him remember the people who loved him, unequivocally, in death and sadness.

She would not sing the melancholy songs of the church to Harrison this time; he would have opportunity enough to learn them later.

Instead, she sang a ballad from another time, something not of the church, and not of the hereafter. An earthbound lament, a universal sorrow; she barely whispered its melody to him over the heavy dirges of the congregation:

The hours sad I left a maid,
A lingering farewell taking,
Whose sighs and tears my steps delayed,
I thought her heart was breaking . . .

Dorcus' Roses

The ancients believed Sirius, the Dog Star, rising with the sun, added to the heat in late summer, hence the term "dog days." Before I learned that, I accepted the old mountain notion that when the heat was so unrelenting it made dogs go mad. I could believe it, but I wondered where they would find the energy. In my observations, dog days in the mountains were always lethargic times, when it was a struggle to simply make it through the day without collapsing from heat stroke, and no one made any extraneous effort to do anything.

It was such a blazing, debilitating day when Foster Thacker, who worked in the Pupil Transportation Department near my office, dropped in before going to the Pike County Fiscal Court meeting. Foster was a somewhat shy, but very friendly man with an ever-present smile and a generosity matched by his ample belt line. In addition to his duties as school bus driver-trainer, he was also the elected magistrate for the district that included Greasy Creek.

Magistrates are the county commissioners in Kentucky and the board they serve on is known as the Fiscal Court. It is an antiquated term, dating from the time the governing body of the county had a judicial function. Their function now is strictly administrative: roads, water, sewer, etc. A County Judge/Executive, who no longer acts in a judicial capacity, but yet attempts to control an often-acrimonious Court, oversees it. Many people in Eastern Kentucky refer to their magistrates as "Squires," or more phonetically, "Square," an obvious mispronunciation of a term left over from the 1700's, when Kentucky became a state and English culture was still pervasive in America. It is typical of most of Kentucky's government structure, with one foot planted in the past and another hesitatingly planted in the present.

Very few magistrates refer to themselves as Squires, as if they are aware of the anachronism. Foster was also modest about his position, unlike his Eighteenth Century predecessors and would not have done well in politics of that period anyway. He had the requisite girth, but I could not envision him in white stockings and a powdered wig.

"Your cemetery's on the agenda today," he said. "Is everything okay now with you and the DOT?"

Foster was well aware of the skirmishes I had with that government agency over the unknown graves in the Old Prater Cemetery, as was the rest of the Pike County Fiscal Court. One of the minor duties of fiscal courts in Kentucky is the responsibility for protecting abandoned cemeteries and graves. Anyone or any entity proposing to disturb an unattended grave has to obtain permission from the Fiscal Court. I had not known the KYDOT was ready to approach the fiscal court and I appreciated Foster checking with me before registering his vote.

"Yeah, I guess," I said. "They agreed to give me an archaeologist, finally."

"Well, I thought I'd check before we voted," he said, and turned to leave for his meeting at the Pike County Courthouse.

"So it comes up today?" I asked.

"Supposed to," he said over his shoulder as he left. "I'll let you know if anything special happens."

So, this is it, I thought. They're finally going to move the cemetery and all this will be coming to an end.

It's about time.

At least the cemetery is going on the National Register now and they'll have to do it right. At least I'll find some of the graves, maybe identify some of them.

But only on the Old Prater, I reminded myself.

I still grieved that I could get no assistance for the Samuel Robinson Cemetery, where there were only seven intact graves. From my research, I had learned there were as many as twenty graves in the past and how many more before their markers sank into the earth along with the unrecorded lives of their occupants?

They're going to miss a hell of a lot of history, I thought. I'm going to lose a hell of a lot of family I never knew I had. But I can't really blame the KYDOT that much, they have a job to do. It's still my fault. I should have taken time to learn more about my family when Rissie was alive, or Paw Pete.

Like they say, youth is wasted on the young, and I pretty much wasted mine.

For over five years, now approaching six, I had been at odds with the KYDOT. It proved to be much like every other Kentucky bureaucracy, terrified of making any accommodation that wasn't political (there were plenty of those), afraid of the slightest transgression of standard operating procedure. It took a judiciously placed newspaper story to get them even to agree to giving me an archaeologist when I wanted an anthropologist, someone who could tell me something about the bones, tell me something I could use to help find my family.

But I had no fight left anyway. After countless hours of doing the research the KYDOT should have done, I was exhausted, bone-tired. Moreover, I was weary of being reminded of what a prodigal son I had been. I was tired of reminding myself that I could have done so much more for my family had I been more responsible in my youth, when all the information I had struggled so hard for in the last five years could have been mine for the asking. And now there was nothing more I could do, except be there when the graves were moved and make sure the KYDOT would treating those hallowed spots with at least some sense of decency.

After work, I went over to Greasy Creek as I usually did before I went home, to feed Mom's cats and wind her grandfather clock and try to maintain the illusion of life in a house that was slowly dying. Since my sister lived in

Tennessee, my brother and I shared responsibility for main-taining the house after Mom came home and went into assisted living in Pikeville. But in truth, Paul did more work than I did on the house, since he lived close by. I tried to come over as often as I could to relieve some of the pressure on him for maintenance and security, but I also simply wanted to sit in the house and remember the simplicity of my childhood and the total lack of fear I had for the future.

The KYDOT had begun buying the final rights-of-way on Greasy Creek for the new road, and some of the maps Paul had acquired were strewn across the kitchen table. I sat down and looked through them again, not quite believing that the cemetery, the whole Snake Branch hollow, and nearly the entire world I knew as a child would soon be covered under a million tons of earth and rock.

My parents' house and the building next to it would remain, but the KYDOT was buying everything else in Snake Branch, including the old house that Rissie and Harlen built when they left their honeymoon cabin in Uncle Will's hollow.

That house was not much bigger than the cabin they first lived in; just four rooms, but it had a grand front porch that extended the width of the house. It had a small back porch too, but the front porch was where the socializing went on, and there was plenty. The house was always crowded with young people, always noisy with their voices. There was something about Harlen and Rissie that beckoned to them. Their irrepressible happiness, the warmth of their home, the shared assurances of their love taught gentle lessons. From Harlen's example, the boys learned that hard work had its rewards and from Rissie, the girls learned that love had its blessings. For years, their home was a magnet for the love-struck and those who wanted to be.

One of my neighbors recalled parties at the house during the 1930's, when she was growing up. Rissie would deep-fry doughnuts and sprinkle powdered sugar over them to feed the adolescent appetites of the kids of the creek who came up on Saturday nights. In summer, Rissie would make buckets of tea during the day and seal it tightly in glass jars, which were dropped into the well to cool until the guests arrived. Electricity had not yet arrived on Greasy Creek, and ice was available only if the ice wagon had come to the camps that day.

In winter, however, there was plenty of ice and the boys would chop up the huge icicles that formed on the rock cliff at the mouth of the hollow to freeze homemade ice cream. Harlen and the boys would salt down the shards in a hand-cranked ice cream maker, awaiting the ambrosia Rissie was preparing in the tiny kitchen under the watchful eyes of her acolytes. Rissie would stir up the mixture while instructing them on the proper quantities of eggs, milk and sugar. She would pour out the exact amount of precious vanilla extract, and her girls' eyes would widen as it was stirred into the thick, pale yellow liquid. And all their mouths would water as it was poured into the ice cream maker. *"Not too fast,"* Harlen would tell the boys, as *they cranked the machine in shifts. "Slow and steady. That'll do it."* When the process was complete, and the cold, rich solid was scooped out of the cylinder, everyone felt they had a part in making it.

If there were no ice, there was always the possibility of dark, brown fudge, boiled hard in Rissie's cast-iron kettle, sometimes with kernels of black walnuts whose hulls had stained yellow the fingers of the boys who brought them to Rissie's doorstep.

After the treats were prepared, they would all adjourn to the tiny living room to listen until dawn to the battery-powered radio that Harlen had bought. From distant cities, places nearly unimaginable to the assembled group, they would listen to Tommy Dorsey or Glenn Miller, and sometimes, after glances were exchanged, couples would drift outside to hold each other as the music permeated the hollow, gliding on the soft, damp summer air. Rissie would go outside at times and observe the glow of the lovers' cigarettes on the porch or in the yard, but she never bothered them when they slipped out to the porch to "smoke." She knew they really went out to spark, but she trusted her charges, or maybe just understood them; Dorcus had taught her that some forces in nature are inalterable.

Times were bad, and there was not much money since the Greasy Creek mine shut down, but Harlen always found work and Rissie worked equally hard in saving what he brought home, and they could afford an occasional luxury to share with the kids of Greasy Creek. In summer, those kids, all of whom she had known since birth, would not miss a chance for her doughnuts and sweet tea. And the chance, of course, the opportunity, to go out on their big front porch to dance with each other in the moonlight as lightening bugs streamed in and illuminated the lovers with their Paphian light. Even in winter, bundled in coats to fend off the chill, the front porch still creaked with couples who would give up the fireplace for the steady radiation of their lovers' bodies.

But the house became quiet after Harlen died and Rissie moved away. Frank and Laura bought the place from her and the heartbroken teenagers followed Rissie down to the big camp house that became the heart of the Hopkins family for another forty years. When Frank moved into the little house, he brought his own memories with him, locked in a trunk where he kept the minutia of his life with Ethel. Laura remembered Ethel and her beauty, and how lost Frank was when he came to her. There could never be the same passion between Frank and her, she knew. She could never compete with a ghost.

It was still a warm house, comforting and secure, with the rich smell of Laura's boiled coffee lingering all day, but it did not have the limitless joy it had before. Frank had too much invested in the past, and waited, somewhat impatiently, for the day he could rejoin his first wife. Laura knew that, accepted it, and quietly raised their daughter as best she could.

But it was never the same anywhere on Greasy Creek. A year after Harlen died, the country was plunged into war and no house in America was the same. There were too many missing faces when the war ended; too many unexpected ghosts from untold stories of violence and death all over the world. Even Glenn Miller was gone, missing somewhere off the French coast. And Greasy Creek had lost its innocence, along with the dreams of the couples who danced among the fireflies on Rissie's porch.

As I walked up the road to the old house, I wondered again about another war, in another century, the first war to come to Greasy Creek, when it wasn't Germans or Japanese who were the enemies. It that war, it was the young men themselves who sought to kill each other and on too many occasions, they did. *At least this house's memories were not sullied by something like that, I thought.*

Frank died in 1973 and Laura lived there alone for another eighteen years. My father bought the house from Ima Jean's family after she passed away, soon after Laura died. Since his death, we had leased the house to a neighbor who maintained it and rented it out for a small profit, when his renters paid him. But with talk of the road coming through Snake Branch, there was no one living there now and I decided to walk up the hollow to look at it again.

From a distance, it looked much the same as it always did: a small, wood-sided house with a rough rock chimney in the middle and a deep, high front porch running the width of the house. The siding was painted white and the house was trimmed in green, almost a match for the moss on the roof, and it had a tall set of concrete steps. At the left of the porch was the well Harrison dug for his daughter and son-in-law, and to its right was the great buckeye tree under which Harrison's funeral was preached. Frank had not changed the house much since Rissie lived there, except for adding the concrete steps to replace the wooden ones that were constantly rotting in the shade of the buckeye, and boxing in the back porch for a bathroom.

But there was a change in the place that I had difficulty in quantifying. Frank's bee gums were missing, but they had been gone for thirty years. Laura gave them away after Frank died, and the hillside where he worked his bees was kept mowed. The old coalhouse was gone, but it had been torn down after we installed gas heat in the 1960's. The great rock wall along the creek bank was still intact, but there was a new drain tile to replace the sagging wooden bridge that once spanned tiny Snake Branch.

Rock walls were common at one time on Greasy Creek, as the early settlers attempted to create flat space to live on from the narrow, sloped land nature provided. But nature also provided plentiful building materials for such structures, and giant stacks of intricately placed rocks, painstakingly erected stone by stone, once dotted the upland gardens after pioneers spent entire summers clearing the land. I hated to see the bulldozers cover them up, as they would when road construction began. They were among the few tangible reminders of another age, of the tenacity of the people who created homes from the wilderness that Greasy Creek once was. In a way, they were the memorials, perhaps the only memorials beside the gravestones themselves, to countless lives of hard labor and simple dreams.

I thought I could account for all the differences since Frank and Laura lived there, but something was missing. There was a curious dissonance surrounding the place, one similar to what I heard, or did not hear, after Laura sold the bees. After I sat down on the steps and surveyed the yard, it came to me: *Dorcus' roses were gone.* In the years that strangers had lived in the house I had never been there, and sometime during that interval, the roses along the upper edge of Frank's yard, where his bees worked so joyfully, had vanished.

When Harlen completed their home, Rissie did for it what Dorcus did for Harrison's a generation before. She went down to the old place at the mouth of the hollow, where steam still rose from the ruins after a rainstorm, and broke off stems from the sprawling rose bush that Dorcus had planted for her son, and brought them back to the hillside next to the house. She planted them in at least three locations, for they still grew there when I was growing up, filling the air with their aroma and covering the ground with their petals when the season was over.

Now I knew of no more such roses on Greasy Creek, except for the bush rambling its way through the tree at the edge of my mother's lawn. They had disappeared from the cemetery, from Rissie's house in the Greasy Creek camps, from this hillside where I brought Charlene to meet Laura and took their pictures while they sat under the rose bush. Charlene was wearing an oversize pink hat as Laura smiled beamingly at me. She was pleased that I had brought Charlene up to meet her. Of my three wives, Charlene became Laura's pick, I suspect, because Rissie had co-opted the previous two, and Laura felt she had better select one before I married someone else. She still had that photograph on her mantle when she died.

So where had the roses gone? After the Civil War, Dorcus and young Adelaide Phillips planted them all over Greasy Creek. It was a way to beautify the graves of those lost in the war, and to give the survivors some comfort as they went on without their loved ones. After Joseph Hopkins' death in 1864, and Zachariah Phillips' death a year later, Dorcus had become the rock for both families, the dependable older sister who took care of the widows and orphans the War had made. In her own house, she raised Haley's children and taught them to remember their mother, and remember their mother's grave with flowers.

Her roses, tough and resilient and unearthly beautiful, were always nearby; they were the modest gifts she gave her chicks and their wounded dams, in a day when there was little else to give and beauty was scarce and dear. And now the only roses remaining of Dorcus' endeavor, at least the only one I knew of, was the climbing bush at the edge of my mother's yard, and would it soon discern that there were few Hopkins left to appreciate its blooms? Would it too wither and die?

All the rest had, probably when the Hopkins or Phillips or other families they once served were no more. When people stopped visiting the Old Prater, its bush waned and disappeared; when Laura died and only strangers came into the house on Snake Branch, the roses in the yard vanished. And with no one living in my parents' house, how long would the last of Dorcus' roses survive?

Was there some part of her soul in those rose bushes, I wondered? Did she plant them to look out for her children even after her death or as reminders to love each other, to look out for each other? Was there some contract I had been a party to by being born a Hopkins, by being Marvin's son, and had I failed to do my part?

Of course I had failed. I had not seriously listened to Rissie, to Paw Pete, to all the old folks when they told me about the Old Ones. Why had I been such so selfish, so colossally self-centered when I was young?

All youth are stupid in that regard, I told myself, they never appreciate their own mortality. But it was of little comfort; it was not my mortality at issue here. It was the soon-to-be or already lost memories of my ancestors.

There is a watershed moment in the process of growing up when you first realize you have but little time on this earth, and that the time of everyone you love on this earth is also prescribed, and there is nothing you can do to prevent it. The enormity of that realization is inexpressible, but it makes us adults. A poet whose surname I share said it best in another country, in a different time, when he ended his most famous poem with an austere line, *"It is Margaret you mourn for."*

But what about me at fifty-six, when my youthful rites of passage were long past? I had no concern for my final resting-place; it was not my ultimate death that troubled me. It was simply that there were once real people, "blood" as my cousin Esther would call them, people who lived and breathed and loved, and would be unremembered, ignored, discounted, and I could not find them.

The question returned again for me: why was I given this task? How could I do a job I was grossly unqualified for? How could I begin to comprehend what had happened here in this valley? Wars upon wars, pestilence, fire, flood, disease, death, all the events of a lifetime, of a dozen lifetimes, of a thousand lifetimes, and precious little did I know of it. The Hopkins family had come here one hundred eighty years before, and I had lived not one-third of that time, and most of those years were spent in a self-imposed, egotistical darkness. In the past five years, I had learned much, but it was a fraction of what I could have learned, should have learned, and would never learn now.

My family and friends were right, I thought, I had become obsessed. I was the last of a line that had always protected others in life and in death: Dorcus, Harrison, Rissie, and my father, all of them did their duty until they died. Dorcus even reached beyond the grave with her roses, her reminders to her descendants. Perhaps even Elisha, when he built the meetinghouse on the gap, knew that memory is frail and had to be protected. And now it would all be over and I had not done my part.

It seemed late in my life for an epiphany, but for the very first time since my father died, on my grandmothers' porch in the shadow of the Buckeye that shielded the mourners at Harrison's funeral, I put my face in my hands and wept.

The next morning, I went to work as I usually did, intending to drop by Foster's office to find out how things went at the Fiscal Court meeting. I had barely sat down with the day's paperwork when the telephone rang. It was a voice of a friend from the KYDOT.

"Hey, Bruce, are you still going to be there when they take up the graves?" he asked.

"Every day," I replied. "I've got eighty-one sick days and I'm gonna use them all."

"Well, that's a good idea," he said. "Because they're not going to give you an archaeologist."

Those words sent a sub-zero chill coursing through my veins. In the five years since I learned the road project would take my hollow and my cemetery, I had never heard anything so shocking, so absolutely wicked and evil.

"Say what?" I said.

"They're not going to give you an archaeologist," he repeated.

"Why not? You guys agreed to that."

"I dunno. I just heard the cemetery was not going on the National Register so they will proceed as they normally do."

Those sorry sons-of-bitches, I thought. I have just been screwed.

"So why isn't the cemetery going on the National Register?" I asked.

"I dunno. That's just what I heard."

"Who made this decision? Was it local or in Frankfort?"

"Frankfort," was his reply.

"Gimme a number," I told him. "I'm going to find out just what the hell happened."

They lie to me, I thought, go to Fiscal Court, get permission to move the graves, and then tell me to go piss up a rope.

They picked the wrong time to do this to me. The absolute, wrong God-damned time in my life to do this to me.

In Frankfort, my call was unexpected; they had obviously not anticipated I would learn so soon of their decision. The KYDOT archaeologist struggled to come up with a response to what I was now demanding of them. I asked him the same thing I asked the local KYDOT: "Why wasn't my cemetery going on the National Register?"

"Well, uh, we hadn't really nominated the cemetery for the National Register," he said. "We, uh, had just talked about it and you didn't supply us with any documentation."

"Documentation? Nobody asked me for any," I said. "I can give you a truckload of documentation anytime you want it.

My temperature was rising now, white-hot, but I suppressed my anger.

Play it cool, I told myself. Don't blow up like you did when you saw what they did to Uncle Will's grave. Don't let these sons-of-bitches see you squirm.

"What about the surveys?" I asked.

"What surveys?"

"The two different surveys that said the cemetery qualified," I said.

He doesn't know that I know, I thought.

"They didn't need any documentation from me when they made their recommendations," I added.

"Uh…well…uh, we still don't have any proof there is anything historic about that cemetery." He was grasping for an answer.

"Really?" I asked sarcastically. "I guess the three Civil War soldiers don't mean anything. Or the two soldiers who died in defense of their country in World War II; they don't count either. Or the fact the cemetery was the founding spot for the Greasy Creek Old Regular Baptist Church. Or the probability the first Hopkins settlers in Pike County are buried there."

He said nothing in reply.

"So you'll come in, dig up whatever is marked and forget about the rest of the graves?"

"Oh, no," he finally said. "We'll remove any additional graves that we find."

"But you're not going to look for any."

"Well, that's not really our job."

You are lying through your teeth, I thought.

"You know, I've read the law on this," I said. "And the way I read it, it says that it is your job."

There was yet another pause on the other end of the line.

Go for the throat, I told myself. Show them you mean business.

"And my attorney agrees," I added.

"So you have some documentation that may be relevant?" he finally asked.

"I can give you whatever you want," I said.

"Well, let me talk to my people again, and we'll see what we can do."

"You'll call me back," I asked.

"Of course, we'll take another look."

"You have my number, right?" I asked.

"Yeah, sure," he said, and hurriedly got off the telephone.

You lying bureaucratic asshole. You're not going to call me back. You're going to dig up my cemetery and leave without looking for a single grave that isn't marked.

But this time, by God, you're not going to get away with it.

After I hung up the phone, I started to put together a war plan. I would plaster this treachery over every news outlet in Eastern Kentucky. Then the telephone rang again. It was a reporter from the local newspaper. He had done a story on the cemetery before and had covered the previous day's fiscal court meeting. He wanted to know if I knew about the fiscal court decision and was I ready for the cemetery to be moved?

"Actually, I'm not," I told him. "I just found out the KYDOT is not going to give me an archaeologist like they promised, and I'm not going to let these pricks toss some dirt into a body bag and say that's my ancestor and haul it away."

He was surprised at my answer, and the venom with which I offer it.

"So, what are you going to do?" he asked.

"I'm not sure yet," I told him, and I wasn't. This development was too stunning for me to fully contemplate. "But you can be assured I'm going to make this KYDOT bullshit public."

"Uh, I can't use 'bullshit' in my story. I can't use 'pricks' either."

"Fair enough," I said, clearing my throat. "Try this instead. If the Kentucky Department of Transportation does not treat my cemetery with the respect it is due, the respect any Eastern Kentucky cemetery is due, and has not gotten even though the law requires it, then I will take whatever action necessary to make sure it does. This will include all legal measures at my disposal, up to and including seeking an injunction in federal court to stop the project. I will not allow them to dig up some dirt, toss it into a body bag and say they've moved the grave."

I could hear him scribbling on his note pad. I waited for him to finish.

"Got that?" I asked.

"Yeah, I can use that."

After we hung up, I put my plan in order. I would contact all the news media I could. From years of working in journalism, I had many contacts and I would call in every IOU I ever had to publicize this thing.

Wait a minute, I thought. I don't have to call in any IOU's. The press will jump on this; it'll sell itself. But then another thought occurred to me: why did I get that last phone call? What prompted that reporter to call me at the almost the exact moment I hung up from the KYDOT?

Coincidence? I'd had a lot of coincidences since I started this work. Too many for mere chance.

Did you have anything to do with this, Lige?

Did you send some ghostly signal to that young reporter to call me just as my blood was ready to boil over? Did your spectral hand move his to the telephone to call my number at the exact moment that I was declaring war?

Do ghosts have that much power?

I pondered the question for only a minute and went back to work. By the end of the day, I had completed my plan and began contacting the press. I called the local television station, radio stations, newspapers; every media outlet I could think of. They were delighted; they all ran stories on my fight.

My next step was to go to the Pike County Fiscal Court and ask them to rescind permission to take up the unknown graves. That had never been done in Kentucky, but I asked Foster to help me and he said he would. Some of his ancestors might be buried on the Old Prater Cemetery as well.

And another thing: I would not be satisfied with the KYDOT merely sending an archaeologist to help me with the Old Prater. I wanted more. I would demand a forensic anthropologist for both the Old Prater and the Samuel Robinson Cemetery as well. I would find all the graves if I had to go to federal court to do it.

How I would do it was problematical, I knew, but somehow I would get it done. I had lost too many skirmishes before; I had to win this one, I had to win this war.

I needed some more ammunition. I was a Risk Manager; I dealt with the law every day and I knew I needed proof of discrimination; that was a necessity. Moreover, if I went to federal court and asked for an injunction, I might have to post a bond. Mentally, I began calculating how much it would cost me and if I could get a second mortgage on my house to pay for it. I needed a smoking gun to prove discrimination, but oddly, I was not anxious. I felt that somewhere, somehow, I would find it. It was if something whispered assurances in my ear, like a father would whisper to his son that he could hit a home run while his Little League friends watched.

And the next week, it fell into my lap.

When I picked up one of the morning statewide newspapers, I found a small story about a cemetery in wealthy Northern Kentucky that was being moved for road construction. It was a minor story, nothing that qualified for the front page, but I learned that the KYDOT was going to spend $26,000 in an attempt to identify five graves that had been abandoned for half a century near Grant's Lick, Kentucky. There was no family to request the research, there was no one who even knew who was buried there, but the KYDOT was going to spend $5200 a grave to find out.

$5200 a grave. They said they couldn't spend a dime on the Samuel Robinson because it had just seven graves, and they are going to spend this much on five at Grant's Lick, wherever the hell that is. But it is in Northern Kentucky, of course, not Eastern Kentucky. History is not important in Eastern Kentucky.

We are second-class citizens here; we're taught that as we grow up. This is where the coal barons kept us in chains for a hundred years, where we have only a tenuous right to squat on our own property and only for as long as the coal companies or the gas companies don't need it. This is where a child is raised to be a good citizen, to find a job and raise a good family, and make a good name for himself, just like in any other place. But he is also taught he can't do it here. He has to go away because there is no work and no future. If he stays here, he gets the leftovers.

Not anymore, I vowed, not for me. They lied to me. This is my family; this is personal. This time I'll make them pay.

I emailed a copy of the story to the KYDOT, and added a friendly note: "I hope this does not indicate institutionalized discrimination toward Eastern Kentucky cemeteries." I did not expect a reply.

Two days later I sent a formal demand for assistance on both the Old Prater and the Samuel Robinson cemeteries, including the services of a forensic anthropologist, citing the Grant's Lick story and recounting the transactions I had up to this point. I sent a copy to the Kentucky Secretary of Transportation.

I expected a reply from that one.

They could not deny the discrimination now.

I had proof.

Wait a minute, I thought, who had given me this proof?

How could such a thing as has just happened occur just as I needed it the most? Why did this story hit the presses just as I was desperately searching for just such evidence?

Damn, Lige, I thought, how did you do this? Did you do this? Who did this?

As the stories hit the presses, the KYDOT found itself answering more inquiries, and I could only speculate at the turmoil I was creating, but I suspected it was having an impact. I proceeded with the next stage of my offensive. The Pike County Fiscal Court was having its first meeting since the KYDOT had gotten permission to move the cemetery and I asked to be on the agenda. The local access cable crew was there to film the meeting as it usually did. I hoped I would give them something more entertaining for their viewers this time.

When I got to the podium I reviewed everything that had happened so far: the surveys of the cemetery for National Registry inclusion, the denial of my request for an archeologist after specifically promising me one, and the money the KYDOT would spend on the Grant's Lick cemetery.

"At this time," I told the Fiscal Court. "I'm just giving you a heads-up. I hope I can settle this with the KYDOT, but if I can't, I'll be back here to ask you to rescind permission to move my cemetery until they agree to do what they should be doing."

The County Judge gently cut me off at that point. "That's all well and good," she said. "But we're going to pass a resolution tonight that says they will extend the same consideration to our Pike County cemeteries that they do in any other part of Kentucky."

The resolution passed unanimously.

It was one of the few issues on which the often-fractious Pike County Fiscal Court had no disagreements among its ranks. That was unusual; perhaps they had visions of their own family cemeteries naked and helpless in front of bulldozers.

The cable company played the tape for two weeks. I had calls at the office and calls at home from people who had similar stories to share. I used them the next week when I went on a local call-in talk show.

"I wanna ask you something," one of the callers said. "How can you sit there and be so cool when the highway department did something like that. If it'd been me, I would've gone down there and kicked somebody's ass."

"Oh, I wanted to," I replied. "But that's what they want you to do. They want you to get mad and act irrationally, because then they can point out what a nut you are and dismiss you. We have to be calm in issues like this, and prepare our cases carefully. Then they have to listen."

My advice was ironic, because the caller could not have imagined the obscenities I wanted to spout at the KYDOT.

Paul had gone with me to the radio station, and sat in the control room as I spoke. I think he was proud of his brother for the case I made without using the "f" word once. On the way home we talked about the cemeteries, about the family, and how it had been our last chance to do something for them. Things like this happen once in a lifetime, and maybe not then, he told me. If I hadn't been there, it would have all been lost, he told me. I had not thought of it that way before. I felt what I had done was pitifully meager compared to what I could have done.

I still had not forgiven myself for my youth.

Within a few days, the KYDOT called to ask for a meeting. The battle was joined.

There were four representatives there when I went into the room, and I did not see much sympathy in their faces. I knew I had caused them trouble; I just didn't know how much. I sat down and waited for them to speak.

"You've requested assistance on the Samuel Robinson cemetery," one of the four men in the room finally said. "It is our understanding that cemetery has been nearly destroyed."

"It may be," I said. "But that cemetery's even more historic than the Old Prater. It contains the graves of Samuel Robinson and Matilda Hopkins Robinson, we know. Matilda was one of the first Hopkins in Pike County. She came here with her father in 1824. Samuel was probably an escapee from the Trail of Tears the Cherokee were put on in 1838 by President Andrew Jackson. The cemetery probably contains the grave of John Miles Hopkins, son of Confederate war hero Joseph Hopkins and probably his sister . . ."

"We're all impressed with your historical expertise," he said abruptly, deliberately cutting me off. "But that has no relevance here. What we're looking at . . ."

"Yes, it does," I replied, cutting him off just as sharply. "And that's your problem. What you don't realize is that if you don't understand history, you won't know what to look for. I know the history of that cemetery, and it's the history of Greasy Creek, of Eastern Kentucky. But you guys don't care about history, do you?"

He ignored my question and went on with the cross-examination.

"I understand that Ola Prater is the oldest living descendant of Samuel and Matilda Robinson," he said, and I immediately

197

knew his strategy. If he could persuade my aunt to not press any claim for services, they could sidestep me altogether. If I were not a direct descendant, I would have no right to make a demand. *Cool ploy, I thought.* But I was ready for that feint as well.

"Oh, she is," I said. "But every Robinson on Greasy Creek is descended from Samuel and Matilda. If they don't know what's at stake here, count on me to tell them."

The Robinsons were a large family. I did not think they would want to deal with half the population of Greasy Creek. Visions of protests and placards waving on the steps of the KYDOT office in Pikeville must have suddenly flashed through their minds.

"So what is it you want us to do?" another asked.

"I want you to find every grave on both cemeteries," I told them simply.

I looked at their faces, which dropped, and then I went on.

"Then I want an analysis made of the remains. I want to know if it is a man or a woman and how old they were when they died. I'd also like to know what might have killed them."

They were shocked, or pretended to be.

"We can't do that. Do you know how much that would cost?" he asked.

I was on a roll now, I knew. I played it for all it was worth.

"Unless it's comes to more than $5200 a grave, I don't give a shit. You did it in Pendleton County; you do it here."

Their faces continued to fall; I issued more demands.

"And I want a forensic anthropologist, not an archaeologist, unless he has specific training in forensics. I want someone trained in this work to analyze what comes out of the graves."

"Where are we supposed to find someone like that?" he said.

"That's your problem. Use the same crew you're using at Grant's Lick."

I began to smell victory. It was sweet. My heart thundered.

"What is it that you really want?" another exasperated KYDOT employee asked me.

"I want equity," I told him. "I want the same thing you're giving to Grant's Lick. I've already done all the preliminary work, the work you should have done to start out with, the work the law requires you do, but that's all right. You didn't do it; I did. That's water under the bridge. However, I want a forensic anthropologist to sift through every grave on those cemeteries."

There was another pregnant pause, and then another spoke: "And if you don't get it?" he asked.

"Try me," I replied. I gave him the most sinister grin I could muster.

I looked at each face of the assembled group in front of me. Perhaps they thought I was some unreasonable prima donna, or perhaps their bosses felt I was, and I realized how untenable was their situation. It could have been they were hoping to humor this madman with glazed eyes confronting them, and realized too late the extent of his lunacy.

How do we get rid of him, they wonder?

But there was something different now in their faces. There was a softening around the eyes, at the corner of their lips. Was it possible that I had touched something inside them, not with my vitriol, but with my reasoning? Is there a point at which you have to quit discarding the past for the future? Had I reached them, finally?

"Look," I said. "I'm not really mad at you guys. I understand you have to follow what Frankfort tells you, and what Frankfort's told you is that they don't want to spend any money up here. Nobody wants to spend any money up here; never have. Historically, the coalfields were written off a hundred years ago. The coal companies, the gas companies, they don't want us to have any identity; they don't want us to have any pride in who we are. They want to keep it simple; keep it the way it's always been.

"What I'm telling you is that that won't cut it anymore, not for me and not for a lot of people like me.

"We've been redheaded stepchildren up here too long; we've been ignored, patted on the head, and told to go away. Well, I'm not going away."

Go for it, I told myself. Take it on home.

"These old cemeteries are all we have left, except for memories, and believe me, they fade. It isn't just for my family I'm doing this. It's for everybody that lives here, for everybody that died here. This is it; this is all we have of our history. The rest has been obliterated, strip-mined, hauled away. We've stood back and taken it for a century because we've been trained to act like second-class citizens, asking for little and picking up the crumbs of whatever somebody else leaves behind.

"Times are changing, gentlemen. I've changed. I used to be just as stupid about the past. I didn't know then and didn't really want to know. Now I do, and I'm not going to settle for anything less."

"Lemme ask you something," one of them broke in, exasperated. "What did you hope to gain from going to Pike County Fiscal Court?"

"Just what I got," I said immediately. "Rescission of the permission they gave you to take up those graves, and you ought to be glad they did. Otherwise, we'd be in federal court right now."

But the rest sat there. The leader of the group, who had said little but had listened intently to what I was saying, then intervened. He knew they had lost, and he knew that I knew, and began to defuse the tension that had mounted. He started to talk about other things and the conversation began to shift. He was younger than me; they all were, but he had seen enough loss in his own experience that he knew what plane I was in, what voice I was speaking from.

These guys weren't crooks, I knew. All four were Eastern Kentuckians like me; perhaps I had finally made my point. Did they really want to play Judas to their own people? Perhaps they realized I was attempting only to slow the undoing of something they could feel a part of themselves, that I was asking only for decency, for a measure of honor for a small part of these ravaged hills at the only time it would be needed. No cold stone on the Annie E. Young Cemetery could ever compensate for what would be lost if the Old Prater was crudely dispatched there. They began to grasp that all I wanted was justice, and after a few more minutes of going over details, the meeting turned pleasant. It was over. They would give me what I asked for.

"Are you pretty well satisfied now?" their leader asked. He had kind eyes. I suspect he had been told to work out the best deal he could for the KYDOT, and he felt he had accomplished his mission.

"Generally," I said. "Although I would like to have it in writing."

"But we all gave you our assurance," another said. "All four of us. Why would you need it in writing?" He was smiling, somewhat patronizingly, I thought.

"Well, remember what happened the last time you promised me an archaeologist?" I reminded him. He remembered, and his smile faded.

"But that's okay, "I said. "Skip the documentation."

His smile returned.

"I'll take your word for it, because if it doesn't pan out," I grinned back at him with only a hint of sinister intent. "I'll start all this all over again."

His smile fell again, but he forced it back and extended his hand. I shook it and said my good-byes. I forced myself to walk calmly and deliberately out the door. I was euphoric: I could not feel the concrete under my feet as I went out to my Jeep.

Looks like we got work to do, old girl, I said as I opened the door and sat down.

"Yes!" I spouted as I high-fived the steering wheel. My hands were trembling as I started the engine and drove back to work.

A few weeks later, as I was mowing my grass for what seemed like the thousandth time that broiling summer, I saw the mailman pull up to my mailbox. I got off the mower and walked out to the road. I had something important there, I knew. There was a formal envelope from the Kentucky Transportation Cabinet. Inside was a letter from the Secretary of the Kentucky Transportation Cabinet himself. It was just less than two pages, formal and courteous on impressive state government stationery.

The Secretary agreed to everything we discussed in the meeting.

I felt unburdened, free, like a draft horse that had just been released from its harness and turned out to pasture.

It was a Saturday and I knew I could finish the grass the next day. I put the letter in my pocket and got back in my Jeep to go to Greasy Creek. I drove through the August swelter toward the Old Prater one more time. I wanted to have the letter with me in case someone wanted proof, even though there were few people on the creek that had any real knowledge of what I had been doing for the past five years, but I expected no questions.

So why did I carry the letter with me? Why did I even feel compelled to go back to the cemeteries? The day was more than half over and I could not have done any work and there was no more work to do anyway. Did I carry the letter in the frail hope some ghostly inquisitor would ask me for proof that the fight was really over? I do not know why I drove; I do not know what force propelled me that day.

The heat was still stifling, but I did not use the Jeep's air conditioner; I wanted to feel the steam as I crossed the Big Sandy; I wanted to taste the heavy air of August. I wanted to remember the moment. Was my tiny victory anything like what Lee felt at Chancellorsville, on a spring day, when he won his greatest victory and lost his greatest general? What had I really won for the cemetery but its destruction?

There were no cars on the concrete bridge at the mouth of Greasy Creek, and I slowed to look over the river. It was not hard to imagine Joseph Hopkins' cotton barges making their way down this desultory stream toward the Ohio, and then the Mississippi, and into the Old South. It was not yet evening, but the mists were beginning to form on its soporous waters, almost as if the river was reaching out to the shore for something to hang onto before night fell, for some security as it gave up its cognition before yielding to sleep.

When I got to the forks of Greasy Creek, I pulled into what had once been Hooker Prater's front yard and parked. I could have driven all the way up to the Old Prater, albeit in four-wheel mode, but even in the heat, I wanted to walk. I could not bring my ghosts this news via a modern conveyance; I had some penance to make this day.

The Old Prater was quiet; I could only hear tree frogs warming up for their evening serenade and the occasional car horn honking in the distance. I wondered if the spirits of the place would even look at me now, since I had agreed to disrupting their rest. There was an awesome stillness to the place, perhaps as it was when the old Greasy Creek mine was running and the great machinery of the mine would suddenly stop. The wives in the town would all cease their work and wait for the whistle to sound, and announce another tragedy. And in no small way, this tragedy had been part of my doing, for I could have fought instead to keep the cemetery intact, to make them move the road instead.

I walked lightly through the recently mown weeds, to Zeke's grave, to Hester's, to Harrison's, to Frank and Ethel's, and to Harlen's at the top of the cemetery. I looked around me, hoping for some phantasmal entourage to have followed me, hoping I could turn to them and say: "Look at this letter. I've got it in writing. They'll do right by you now." But I had no audience for my news; the stones were mute and they all seemed to face away. I waited for a voice, for a touch on my shoulder, for a sign that they approved, but there was nothing.

Before I left the cemetery, I looked at the bare ground where Cornelius and Dorcus were surely buried and realized I would never really locate their graves.

You've returned to the dust, I thought. They won't find anything of you, will they?

I walked down the hill to the weed-shrouded Samuel Robinson Cemetery. Would someone ask me of my accomplishment here? But there was no sound.

Somewhere in there, I thought, is your grave, Victoria, but I don't think I can find you either. I don't think I'll have any more success than Hooker did, looking for Otra. I'm so sorry.

Behind me on the mountain, now barren of trees, the road work had already begun. I clutched the letter from the Secretary in my hand, hoping one last time that someone would ask for the tangible result of my work, but no one did.

If it had been Avery, I thought, he would have set up a redoubt in front of the cemetery and dared the KYDOT to come up the hill into his gunsight.

But I was not Avery, or Caudill, or my father, and I knew all I could do was what Hooker did: collect the stories and tell them, keep faith with the memories. *I promise you that, I thought. I promise you all at least that.*

If there were spirits near me, I did not see them, did not see what disappointment may have been written in their eidolic faces, and I got back in my Jeep and drove up Gardner Fork to do one more job before dark. I parked in Mom's empty driveway and got out to pet the cats that ran to me as they usually did. *At least they're happy to see me, I thought.*

Paul's dogs ran over from his house to play and the cats hissed and scattered in protest. I retrieved my father's ladder from behind the house and carried it to the edge of the lawn, placing it against the tree where Dorcus' rose bush had waned after another summer of brightening the hillside. I started up the rungs.

The dogs were sitting at the ladder's base, staring up into the tree, when my brother pulled into the driveway and came over to me.

"What are you doing up there?" he asked.

"A little project," I said. "I want to start me a rose bush over at my house."

"From these?" he asked questioningly. "You can get roses at Lowe's. They're on sale. You're liable to get killed up there."

"Nah," I said. "I'll be okay. Besides, Lowe's doesn't have these roses."

These were the family flowers, Dorcus' flowers; no home improvement store would have them, nobody in the world would have them. And as for Paul's worry about my safety, I had no fear. Dorcus would not let me fall off that ladder. Or Rissie, or Elisha, or whoever had been guiding me and protecting me for the past five years.

And for how much longer than that, I wondered. Most likely for my entire life, somewhere close by without my knowing it.

I cut sprigs for my brother too, and when I came back down, he helped me pot them. During the winter we would keep them safe and watered, in a window where sunlight would reach them and they would be protected from the chill. Next year, when spring came back to Greasy Creek, we would set them out.

Epilogue: Ghosts

It is the end of summer now, and the few gardens still tended have peaked. Their caretakers have put aside the hoes for another season, yielding the fight to the horseweeds and cicadas. The summer produce, what there was of it, has been eaten, or consigned to the freezer or, more rarely, the once-ubiquitous Mason jar. All that remains is the occasional tomato not yet devoured by turtles and the rows of mustard greens and turnips awaiting the first frost. It is, of course, not enough to sustain a farm family, but there are no real farms on Greasy Creek anymore. There are only the small gardens, near the houses, where retirees can put on overalls and till the earth and consult the signs and pretend to be the farmers their ancestors, whose survival depended on their bounty, truly were.

These gardens are enough for those who prize their vegetables, but it is not just for food that compels these neoteric farmers to put something in the ground every year. They plow and plant and weed and hoe for a different reason, one not fully expressible in the noon sunlight. They are proud of their worn tools, and cast off their eroded hoes with great reluctance, and proudly share their beans with their neighbors. All the while they deprecate the product of their labors, even though the food they have grown is the only real thing, except for their children, that is indisputably of them and them alone.

The modern gardeners of Greasy Creek have no turning plows brightly polished by the earth and no stoic mules to pull

207

them. The great blades that furrowed the soil have long been consigned to the back of the shed where snakes and spiders commune; their owners have no use for them. The motorized tillers they use instead are but noisy substitutes for the crack of leather reins on the back of a reluctant beast. The ersatz farmers of Greasy Creek, with modern seductions to lure them away from the fields, have little time to break new ground, and even less need. But they garden anyway, and know they must; it is somehow obligatory, and unconsciously they do it as remembrance, as duty to a past not fully appreciated.

And when the days grow short, they can sit on their porches, for porches have returned to Greasy Creek, and look out over their gardens, exhausted and resting for another year, in respectful tribute to a harsher, but somehow kinder way of life.

It is the languorous season, here at summer's end, and life has slowed. The creek no longer threatens to pour out of its banks as it does in early spring, when all passions are aroused, and is reduced to a trickle. There is just enough water to render a sweet cacophony to lull the early sleeper who has tired of his labors and turned off the television set and the air conditioner and opened the window to catch the breeze.

Dusk comes earlier now; and longer evenings afford more time to total the year's accounts. The gains and losses, the victories and defeats, the crises and their denouements are no longer urgent, and no longer carry the weight they did when the year was young and the blood was hotter. Now only peace is desired, and if unobtainable, at least rest.

Through the open window, some lingering fragrance of summer can be detected, even if it is only a false memory locked in an errant synapse and released weeks after the flower is gone. The perfume attending the season, as seductive as the prospect of sleep itself, is nearly intoxicating for tired bodies and weary minds, both to be assuaged by the somnolent cowls gliding across their beds. From somewhere they detect the final burst of lilac, the closing movement of a symphony of roses, and the last riot of honeysuckle, palliating the senses, forgiving all sins, and annealing the dreams of the most restless sleeper, and they are freed of the year's commitment.

I've done all I can this year, they say before they sleep. What I missed, I'll do next year, they say. They are not concerned; there is always another year to finish the porch or patch the roof; and there will always be time to plant a garden. It is no sin to leave work unfinished; the opportunity will come again. Except for those whose opportunity cannot come again, who have no time left.

I am of the latter category; my opportunity is gone, and I know it. This is why I am on this hillside for the last time in my life. My work must stand, regardless of its conclusion. There is an awesome finality to this day, unlike any other day I have ever lived, and I pray I was successful.

It is not merely a summer that ended today. I am fifty-six years old, and for nearly six years, one-tenth of my conscious life, the patch of torn ground I am visiting has been my albatross and my salvation, my unflagging companion awake or in dreams, and now it no longer matters. Now there is no driving compulsion, no fever, no midnight epiphanies; my pursuit is ended. There is nothing more I can do. The moving finger has writ, the poet says, and moved on.

I am alone again on the cemetery, or at least what was once the cemetery. There are only mounds of dirt, some of it the dark humus, the topsoil of a hundred thousand years of decay and some the maternal yellow clay from further down, all stirred and blended and, pushed here and there until finally abandoned. I am alone, except for the sorrow, and I have come here for the last time in my life, to the place where my ancestors slept, because the bulldozers will begin their work in the morning and erase even the contour of this hill.

The men who moved the stones and sifted the graves and secured whatever detritus they could of what was once men and women and children have finished their grisly toil and are gone. The archeologists have done their work, noted all the evidence, and submitted their final reports. The graveyard, and whatever remained of the mortal coils once buried here, now sits elsewhere, in a clean, well-tended place with weedless avenues, where the graves lie in precise alignment, unlike the scattered mounds and forgotten faces this cemetery once closed over.

And the appalling question remains; whom did I miss? What life once led in this narrow valley will not be accounted for in the new place? What dust of mine will have no stone to watch over it for another unfulfilled promise of eternity?

In abject humility, I apologize to the souls I have left behind, if indeed I have left any, and I am overtaken by weariness.

In search of a familiar place to rest, I look for a landmark amid the ruin, and find none. With no compass to guide me, I pick a spot. It is here, I believe, Union soldier Ezekiel Prater was laid to rest a hundred years ago. The tree that grew there and pushed my great-great-great grandfather's government-issue tombstone to one side is gone; as are all the trees, including the great cedar Harrison planted to mark Lila's grave. There is nothing now to offer me shade, but the sun, ruthless in August, has peaked, relented, even failed, and the winds are rising and falling through the valley. Like coy schoolgirls, they touch my face and run away, I feel their touch and they disappear.

Schoolgirls once played down there, in the schoolyard that now stands empty in front of me, on the valley floor Elisha once owned. The school year has begun, but the Greasy Creek School was closed in spring, a casualty of declining enrollment, and for the first time in a century no voices will rise to the cemetery.

Just as well. No one to listen anyway. The Hopkins and the Praters no longer sleep here.

The warm air of the valley, locked in by the daytime sun, is freed now from its bonds, and it lifts my gray hair as it escapes up the mountain. Behind me, perhaps cooled by the open graves, the heavier air falls against my shoulders, and slips under the warm zephyrs, pushing them higher as it races to the schoolyard.

What was it like down there, before the school was built? Not that nondescript brick structure, which has been there a mere four decades, an inconsequential blink in time, and not even the other school, the sagging wooden barn with three rooms and oiled floors that I attended, as did my father before me, and my grandfather before him. That was Middle Greasy School then, where Marvin Hopkins, star baseball player of the venerable institution, saw Pansy Prater of the Upper Greasy School knock one of his pitches clear out of the field and fell in love with her before the ball hit the ground. A generation before him, Frank Hopkins picked up the doll dropped by Ethel Coleman on the same field, brushed it off tenderly before returning it to her, and never let her smile leave his mind for the rest of his life. The schoolyard was Juliet's garden for how many swain of Greasy Creek?

But I speak of further back, when no school occupied the rare flat ground of this valley, what stories could be told? What was there on the field bounded by the waters of Greasy Creek on one side and Gardner Fork on the other? A pasture? Pens for cattle, probably. Certainly a house for Sally and the children since this was where Harmon raised his family and he was the oldest child of Sally and Elisha. Of course, they were never legally wed, I remind myself, as if that held any consequence for Ol' Lige. They were all his wives, I know, with or without the trappings of ceremony.

But something happened here, in a past not given to me to remember, that drew me back to this place so many times. Will I ever know what called me from Ohio, from Virginia, to this inscrutable weathered point on a nondescript hillside, to look over this distant field so many times, and record in my journals what I have never seen? And why am I denied any confirmation that it happened at all?

Lige, you magnificent bastard, was it you who guided me all this time? Was it Rissie? It had to be you. Tell me now. I must know for I can never again look over this valley from this spot. By this time tomorrow, there will only be the exposed bedrock of the mountain waiting for the drillers and blasters to finish

211

what the earthmovers will start in the morning. There is nothing to stop them now, and I grieve for the people I may have ignored or those I could not find. By daylight, it will be too late and even the outline, the very shade of this hillside will fall, and I cannot rectify my mistakes.

And I will be orphaned forever; I will not have even the stones of my ancestors to touch in the field they were placed when no one thought they would move a mountain just to make a road. Will you not tell me the truth? Will you not tell me at least if I have missed a grave, missed some once-hallowed spot that was never to be forgotten?

But I hear nothing and feel only the wind swirling around me, the warm and the cold, the last of summer and the first of winter, the life and the death. I sense only the eternal cycle played out again, and I find no resolution.

I know there was not always sadness on this hillside. There was a cabin here before there was a cemetery, and two old people lived out their last days here in well-deserved satisfaction. Children, grandchildren, even great-grandchildren visited, and brought food and stories to brighten their days; they were at peace. The sum of their lives was more than enough to compensate for what they gave up in Virginia. More than they would ever have had in Virginia. They could never have owned the land there as they owned the land here. No broad plains or flat meadows exist on Greasy Creek, but the clearings they wrested from the forest had not been claimed by anyone before; they were the first to subdue the land. Their children would always live on that land, and die there, and be buried on it forever. And the sons and daughters of their children would flourish and replenish the earth. In return, they expected little; merely that their graves would always be tended and they would never be forgotten. When they died they were at peace, knowing their memory would be restored by the hearthside forever.

Or so they thought. And it was left to me to acquiesce in the destruction of that memory. Would they have been so happy if they had known what would become of this place, if they had known there would be no reason to remember in just a few generations? And that their irresponsible great-great-great-great grandson would have been charged with the most awesome responsibility of all their descendants?

Could I have done anything more?

How grand it must have been to live when they did, before the War, of course. There had to have been a joy to life then: the toil and sweat of summer giving way to the joys of fall, of the harvest, of another year of prosperity; inconceivable to anyone of this life, where every day another mountain tumbles into the valley it once protected.

It would have been just this time of year that Lige would have celebrated, thrown a party, a mountain soiree where he could strut and preen and show off his success. Being the oldest son, he was the heir apparent, and it would have been his responsibility to gather the clan to honor his parents. Just to mark a year of good fortune, as every year had been since he walked here with his father from Old Virginia.

For nearly forty years, the Hopkins family had grown and prospered on Greasy Creek, as Cornelius expected they would. Although Elisha now owns most of the creek, and his father still lives in the cabin he built near the river at the mouth of the creek, he has brought his father to this field today to celebrate all their successes. There was always a reunion, a gathering of the clan every year, a display of the proceeds of Cornelius' gamble. And every year, even with his sight dimming, the year was brighter than the year before, and the old man could see his clan enriched by another season, and he was happy.

It would have been a grand party in 1860, probably the grandest of them all, and it was the last for the clan, although they did not know it. Joseph's cotton farming venture, backed by his brother, was a great success. All the children were successful, with rich, full lives, their own farms and children tumbling over each other. Elisha had accumulated three families to present at the gathering, and they were all his children, all his blood, regardless of their dams.

And altogether they eat at the family tables. All the clans: Hopkins, Robinson, Blackburn, Adkins, Coleman, Phillips, Thacker; all the peripheral clans, all the families, all supping with Cornelius, the founder, and Elisha, the heir, all suspecting nothing but increase in the years ahead, all anticipating this summer would return forever.

What would they have eaten, I wonder? The household gardens would have been in so there would be plenty of corn and beans, but it would be too soon for hog-killing. There would always be fried chicken, but Elisha would want something special this time, something more festive. A fish fry, maybe? That would fit the bill, and Elisha would order his sons to the river to catch catfish and bass and bring them back in barrels to stock his pond. He would have directed the women to begin the fires at daylight, coal-fires instead of wood, to heat the oil in the kettles to boiling by mid-morning. He would have gutted and sliced the fish himself, all the time instructing his sons and daughters on how best to save every morsel even though the river was packed and would always be inexhaustible with fish.

There would be great stacks of cakes and pies for the women and children, and of course, Lige's whiskey, and there was none better, for the men. There would be laughter, and fiddlers, and singing, and above it all, the Elysium of children whose voices, jubilant and unfettered, had never known danger or disappointment or loss.

I can see it plainly, directly in front of me, as if it were happening now, the evening having already passed into morning, but not the insecure morning of tomorrow. Instead, the morning of far yesterdays breaks in front of me, and from my seat on Ezekiel's vacant grave, I can see in indisputable purity what I had only been told of before. It is as if the music of my blood, my bones, the phyletic resonance of my grandsires, has taken leave of my body to gather and rise to a great storm to break over Greasy Creek. And in its wake, the bitter effluvium of one hundred forty-two years is washed away, revealing in high relief the unutterable mystery, the forbidden, indescribable tableau of the past.

"George, God damn it, get off your sorry ass and fetch some coal," says Elisha to his indolent son, sitting barefoot beside the pond waiting for the fish to come up to be snared. "That oil has to boil 'fore we put in the fish." He pronounces it "feesh," as my father did.

"But Paw, I got my good clothes on," George replies.

"I don't give a good God damn," says Lige. "Get over to that coal bank. That ain't women's work, boy. Do it now, or do you want to wait until Victory gets here and do it then?" He calls her "Vic-TORY" instead of "Victoria," as I knew he would.

With this threat, George jumps to his feet; at seventeen, he does not want his cousin to see him catering to the women. He is a man now, and would be crushed if his beloved did not consider him so.

"And bring some more grain; Joe's coming over from Shelby Creek and his horses ain't going to go back hungry," he yells to his son, now hopping on one shod foot, attempting to pull a boot over the other as he races to complete his chores.

"Why you puttin' them God damn brogans on for anyway, boy?" Lige, who loves to laugh, roars at the sight of his gawky boy stumbling off to do the child's work assigned to him before his true love arrives and he can pretend to be a man. "Too proud to go barefoot in front of your lady love? Afraid Victoria will see your big toe?" His laughter rises above the hubbub of the preparations.

By now, the bustle has taken on its own life. Women scurry back and forth, piling food on the tables, shooing flies, and slapping away larcenous young hands trying to pilfer a slice of pie before such treats are permitted.

The older children have other pursuits to stave off their hunger: the boys catch huge red crawdads on the creek bank to rush with to their female cousins, to terrorize them with sinister outstretched pincers. Those cousins, of the same age, but older as women are with breasts appearing and hips flaring, scold

215

their ignorant kin for their childishness, and flee back to their mothers for protection. All in all, it is a typical family affair for the Hopkins clan, and as the routine is established, the guests arrive and the feast begins.

As each brother or sister enters the gate, Elisha greets them. "Come and see Pap," he says as he shakes the hand of the brother or brother-in-law and brings them to Cornelius who sits patiently with his grandchildren at his feet. "Hey, Pap," they say, "Look how the boys have grown," or "Look at my pretty girls." And the old man smiles, and reaches for his children to hug them, to pull them close, to pass on the spirit of his forebears to another generation. Dorcus coos over the youngest, as women do, and the ritual is made over for each house of the clan.

After the tribute, he ushers them toward the tables. "Get some fish now," he says. "Make the little un's watch for bones."

"Great God damn it, Matilda," Elisha says to his sister, who has walked across the creek with her husband from their home. "You look as dry as last year's horse turd. Ain't you and Sam doin' no good?" Elisha, as mischievous as any of his sons, loves to torment her.

"Listen here, Sister," he says. "I'm going to that old Indian a right dram of my special run. He'll have your toes curlin' afore the rooster crows." And he laughs loudly at his sister's discomfiture, as his brother-in-law smiles both at her embarrassment and the prospect of Elisha's liquor.

Presently, Joseph and Lucinda arrive, their mostly feminine brood in tow, with Victoria in the lead. George, who has dusted off his clothes, saunters over nonchalantly to be near her, and attempts with all his self-control to act disinterested. Victoria, blushing and shy at fifteen, keeps her eyes downcast, except for the occasional glance toward her beloved, to make sure he is still there, still waiting with racing heart for the time they can be alone.

And so it goes: each guest, each family member or extended family member is greeted by Elisha, the oldest son, the pleni-

216

potentiary of the father of the clan, and the man they all turn to for advice and counsel.

Soon Zachariah and Clarinda arrive, their new son Joseph in her arms, the loss of the twins, now buried across the creek, still hurtful but assuaged by his arrival. Elisha greets him as a brother, as he is almost as close to his brother Joseph as Elisha, and has proven himself with his loyalty. He hugs Clarinda as the niece she is, and, after speaking to Cornelius and Dorcus, she joins the women preparing the feast, taking her place beside Elisha's wives and children.

There were three wives in 1860, and each have their places. Phoebe is the first, the legal wife, and as such she has the office of authority and directs all the others in preparing the food for the men to eat before the women and children take their seats, as is the custom. Sally, the second, accepts her role meekly, but tells herself she is Elisha's favorite, although she knows it would be anathema to express it. She was the first to lure him away. Let them do what they want, she thinks, when the reels begin, I will put on my shoes and laugh and dance with Elisha in front of everybody.

Haley, the last, chafes at the stricture of this family organization, but goes about her duties without complaint. Elisha was attracted to her by her full body, her animation, by the glow that pulsed from her, by the smile she cast broadly and still does when she sees him. But he has seen a loss of the fire that tinged her eyes and curled around the corner of her lips. She is more subdued, and yet somehow more anxious and Elisha sees it. It has begun to trouble him and he has spoken to her about it, although she dismisses his concern.

I grow tired too often these days, she thinks. Working too hard, but the leaves are turning and we'll soon gather walnuts together, just me and Lige, and he will lay me down on the moss like he did the first time he met me and everything will be well again.

Elisha can read the thoughts of his women, can discern their moods, and knows when they have their snits, but does not react. He has responsibilities this day, and he makes his rounds

217

through the field with his brothers and friends, awash in the topics of men, the politics of the times. For the time being, the women must fend for themselves.

It is an election year, and the presidential election is on everyone's mind. Not long ago, the young Vice President of the United States, a strikingly handsome man with ice blue eyes, stood on this very spot, and told Elisha he was going to make the run.

"John Cabell, you got my support," Elisha offered him, and that meant all of Greasy Creek would vote for John Cabell Breckinridge, and surely the rest of the country would follow suit.

"I thank you, sir," the Vice President replied, extending his hand. "It is a great work ahead of me, and I would not attempt it without the backing of my friends." John Cabell was always close to Greasy Creek, to Pike County, for he knew that he truly had friends there. His grandmother, in fact, was a Hopkins from Virginia, although not of the same clan, still a Hopkins, and still from Virginia. In this golden summer of 1860, John Cabell Breckinridge was welcome on Greasy Creek, and to Elisha as much a member of the clan as anyone.

But there is not all sweetness in this last feast of the year; since John Cabell has come to Greasy Creek, the fabric of the Union itself has come under question. What seemed to be no issue at all for Elisha has erupted into bitterness across the country, and there were strange words spoken recently: secession, states' rights, even war. It will not come to that, everyone agrees. John Cabell is the greatest man running and he will keep the Union together. Cornelius, who was born when the country was born, takes no part in the discussion, and takes no sides on the issue. But the others do, and there is a curious discordance to the afternoon, as Elisha walks through the assembly of brothers and friends.

By the time the food is consumed, and the jugs have been brought out, and the women and children remanded to their own devices, the conversation has grown louder. "I'm just saying we might have to choose sides if old Abe Lincoln is elected," he hears someone say to the resounding curses of his audience. "Ain't no God damn danger," they say. "No chance that ape will beat John Cabell," Elisha hears as he walks toward the group.

"Lige," he is asked. "What do you think? Will the North secede when John Cabell wins it?"

Has it come to this, Elisha wonders? There are always arguments in politics, but since when have we thought the country would tear itself apart over an election? He is suddenly chastened; his words have import and meaning now, beyond the banter, the sometimes-scatological jokes that are his forte. He becomes strangely reticent.

"Well, Lige, what do you say?" But for the first time today, or any day he can remember, he cannot speak. His tongue is suddenly dry, as if he had gone all day without water. A wall has appeared in front of him, between the man and his friends, a swaying wall blackened with soot and blood. Presently, it tumbles down, and like an earthquake breaking under a charnel house, hideous rotted corpses appear where healthy young men once stood.

Something terrible has been revealed to him. He has been shown that he will outlive every man gathered around him, and he is speaking to the dead, although they do not yet know it, and for some, death will come very soon. But all of them, every man now standing upright in his field will be of the spirit long before he will, and he knows he will be haunted by them until he dies.

Elisha knows he must speak, and he forces down the foulness that has risen from his stomach, and croaks a response, begging the questions asked of him.

"What are you boys yapping about?" he asks. "It's just a God damn election. Ain't nobody going to secede. That's just politics." But as he speaks the words, he knows they are lies, and he knows they will never gather here again on this gentle field. He can already see death moving among them, casting horrible visages over them, and he sees them putrefying in their graves, the worms feasting on them as ravenously as these

friends consumed the fish from his table, and he blanches at what he sees.

His brother Joseph appears in his rotted countenance; decayed after a dozen Union bullets rend his body. His nephew Zachariah, dead by only one, that of their cousin Winright standing near him now, still a friend and kinsman, but both of them turning to dust, the corrupted flesh falling away in their coffins. All the others, dead from the war, in the conflagration itself or in the years of recovery, when recovery was never to be had. And that war, not yet declared is now pressing upon them all, and he knows this life, this sweet interlude before the pitch of battle, is lost.

"If war comes," says Joseph, speaking when his brother cannot, "we got to support the South. We got to fight, Lige."

"But will Kentucky stay with the South?" asks Lum. "What has the South ever done for us?"

"You're from the South, boy," Joseph replies. "You're Pap's son."

"But this ain't the South, and Pap ain't there no more," Lum says. "The past don't matter."

But Elisha knows the past does matter and the war will come. He knows Kentucky is too close to the North to side with the South and too close to the South to escape devastation. We will lose regardless; we will lose everything, he knows, but he cannot say this. He can only admonish them for talking too loudly and frightening the women, and again he forces his lips to move.

"You boys are, by Jesus, scaring the hell out of the women. I don't know what's going to happen; I don't care. It ain't up to us. But we're all going to vote for John Cabell and that's that. I don't know if Kentucky will stay with the South if war comes, but I do know it ain't none of our goddamn business. There'll be no one trifle with us here."

He tries mightily and squeezes out a smile; the old Elisha returns, if only in pantomime, and he turns the topic to horses and whiskey. "You boys seen my new stud? Joe, take them over to the pen and show him off. I'm going up to the springhouse to get some more jugs."

The men are startled at Elisha's perfidy, but drift away obediently as he turns to the hillside for his short journey.

"Want me to go with you, Pappy?" George yells to his father from the fence where he is sitting with Victoria.

"Naw, you keep Victoria company," he says, to George's relief.

From my ruined cemetery, I can see all this and hear every word. How is that possible? How can I do that from up here?

Elisha crosses the creek and passes the small cemetery where his sister is buried, and a few children, victims of accidents or summer diseases, have broken the ground with their graves. A few rocks mark the graves of other adults, or a few whitewashed crosses now tilting as the earth settles. This cemetery will fill up when the war comes, he knows. He cannot bury his parents here when their time comes.

By the time he reaches the spring, he knows what must be done. When the War begins, he will bring his parents up to the security of these forks, where he can look out for them. And when they die, he will bury them up here, overlooking the field where there has been so much happiness and reward for him. This place will always be safe for them and for their graves.

Elisha retrieves two more jugs of whiskey from the cold, clear water of the spring. It has been a good year, and his production fills the rock-lined pool inside the tiny house he built with his own hands. Before he begins his descent, he samples both jugs and looks down into the valley. More guests are arriving, and he squints to see who has wandered in.

I stand there and watch along with him, one hundred forty-two years later, as more guests arrive at the gate.

From Old Virginia, Cornelius' brother James has come and with him their father. Never mind that for a decade James has not walked the earth nor has their father for decades longer. But they have made the journey. They have come to this tiny valley at the confluence of two creeks where Elisha has built a *life to pass on to his children at this ethereal moment when no force in the universe can diminish his joy.*

And I am here on this hillside, standing beside my great-great-great grandfather whose last stertorous gulp was forty years before I drew breath. And I see no conundrum in any of this.

Nor does Elisha, standing tall and erect in front of the cabin that has not yet been built, under the trees that have not yet sprouted, and among the shattered graves that have not yet been carved; his great beard ruffled by the wind rising between us. He tenderly places his whiskey on the ground and stares at the field below him as more guests enter the field.

I know them now, everyone, even the ones I have never seen, could never see. They are the Old Ones of Rissie's stories, and I know all their names, and recognize all their faces. They were waiting for me on her porch as I turned to close her garden gate, and they were waiting for me under the cedar that shaded Harrison's grave as I turned around to see the winding cemetery path instead of Rissie's even sidewalk.

There is Dorcus, Elisha's daughter, named for his mother, but stubborn and free-spirited; more like him than any of his sons. She has come with her son who will not be born for seven years. Harrison toddles into his great-grandfather's arms. When he steps back, he is a man and his mouth is whole, the cleft erased by the years, a great mustache growing over the gap no longer visible or consequential. Beside him stands his young wife, dewy-eyed and blushing, with no trace of the fever that will take her from him. Their son Frank is behind them, stepping proudly with Ethel and their children, no poison from the Great War sullying his lungs. My grandmother Rissie behind them, with my father as a child, pink and baby-fatted in the new stroller Harlen bought for him with the money he worked out in the Greasy Creek mine.

There is laughing, teasing, good-natured jostling, a bedlam of joy on this ancient field, and then a noise rises; conversations pause.

At once the valley fills with sound, resonating off its walls. Eyes turn to the road, looking for the source, to a dust cloud rising above the trees. In a moment, something breaks through the pandemonium, and the din is clearer. It is of young men laughing, a tinny radio blaring, and an unmuffled engine growling in the distance.

Amid the dust rising from its red spoke wheels, a shiny blue Plymouth roars into the compound and the doors open. There is my father as a young man looking out from behind the wheel; his endless smile permeating the field. Only my Uncle Avery, getting out the other side, has a wider grin. From the back seat, my cousin Caudill emerges, impatient to join Marvin, his older brother, pressing close to him to learn the ways of men. All of them strong and intrepid, glorying in their youth, faces abeam with laughter, the way I always knew they were, and, in this place, the way they will always be.

From another realm of the earth, one I had no prospect of knowing, Elisha speaks. "They're all here, son," he says to the wind crossing the valley. "Just like you reckoned."

His words are gentle, not at all what I expected them to be, but who could expect to know the ghost of his great-great-great grandfather?

Elisha turns to me as the wind recedes, across the gulf of years, across infinity itself and speaks:

"When you comin' boy?" he asks me tenderly, the glow of his eyes warming me as if it were noontime.

I don't know, old man," I say abruptly and nervously. "I don't think I'm supposed to know."

Elisha roars with laughter, and slaps his knees.

"I always said you was smart," he says.

"It was you all the time, wasn't it?" I ask the ghost. "It was you telling me where to look, where to go. It was you who guided me."

"Well, now," he says easily, a smile at the corner of his lips. "I don't think you're supposed to know that either."

"Did I miss anyone?" I ask. "Will you at least tell me that?"

But he says nothing. With a smile, he catches my eye, and prompts me to look back to the field.

In the pen where the horses are kept, where they munch contentedly on George's offering, there is an impatient brown and white mare, brushing the fence rails, anxious to be freed. I see her clearly, and even without the bridle and saddle she wore the one time I saw her in the passageway at the Pikeville Stock Market, I know her. There is the same pleading in her eyes, the same yearning for my hand on her nose, on her flank, for an apple or a lump of sugar I did not have to give her then.

"She'll be waitin' for you too, when you get here," he says, reading my thoughts as he always has. "Bring her a big red one." And his laughter thunders across the valley.

He picks up his jugs to leave, but pauses and looks at me directly, not unkindly, but without device, and speaks: "Listen, son, I want to tell you something."

I stare at him transfixed and say nothing. What will he say?

"You did good here, boy. You did real good. Don't let nobody tell you different."

And the smile reappears, the one I had seen before on my father's face, or on Rissie's or Frank's or on any of the faces I loved, a smile I had almost forgotten existed, but would never again forget. And he turns away, down the mountain into the fog now rising up from the creek, to depart my dreams forever, and he whistles an old cavalry tune as he passes.

The scene before me melts and disappears, and when it returns, there is only the green flat field in the middle of Greasy Creek where Indians make their campfires. They too, disappear and in sure cadence, houses rise and fall, a church rises and falls, a wooden school is built, then dismantled, and the artless brick structure of today is returned to its place in this now-resolved interstice of time.

I am alone again.

Except for the spirits, of course. I know now they have always been here, always waiting, quietly guiding me with deathless momentum. And they are not without substance. Like the honeysuckle I cannot see, but which intoxicates me, I am enraptured on this ruined mountainside in this failing light. My spirits are powerless but not impotent, for they exert a greater force than I have ever known, could ever know, and I have always been a part of it without my knowing, for there could never be such knowledge.

They will always be here.

Even if the school is gone, and the hills are gone, and the road moves travelers through this place at the speed of light, they will be here as long as the field is there, as it will always be. Not in the temporal, and not even in the abstract, but in a plane not quantifiable by any human measure.

I am finally content.

It is time to go, and tenderly as I would put a child back into its cradle, I break from the gentle wraiths that have clung to my heart for so long.

I slip through the mists of the mountain, imbued with honeysuckle out of time itself, on an old road, and follow my forebears into the valley from whence I came, to make a final peace with my soul and rejoin the earthly remnant of my family.

Printed in the United States
1260800006B/1-51